Attention **D**eficit
*H*yperactivity **D**isorder

Attention Deficit Hyperactivity Disorder

What Every Parent Wants To Know

by

David L. Wodrich, Ph.D.

Clinical Director of Child Psychology
Phoenix Children's Hospital
Phoenix, Arizona

with invited contributors

·P·A·U·L·H·
BROOKES
PUBLISHING CO.

Baltimore • London • Toronto • Sydney

Paul H. Brookes Publishing Co.
P.O. Box 10624
Baltimore, Maryland 21285-0624

Typeset by The Composing Room of Michigan, Inc.,
Grand Rapids, Michigan.
Manufactured in the United States of America by
BookCrafters, Falls Church, Virginia.

Persons described in this book come from composite case studies.
The names of individuals are pseudonyms. Any similarity to
actual individuals or circumstances is coincidental and no
implications should be inferred.

The reader is advised that this volume is not to be considered a
substitute for the professional judgment of a psychologist or
psychiatrist.

Library of Congress Cataloging-in-Publication Data
Attention deficit hyperactivity disorder : what every parent wants
  to know / by David L. Wodrich.
    p.   cm.
  Includes bibliographical references and index.
  ISBN 1-55766-141-3
  1. Attention-deficit hyperactivity disorder.   2. Hyperactive
children—Family relationships.   I. Wodrich, David L.,
1948–   .
RJ506.H9W63 1993
618.92'8589—dc20   93-31107
                                                         CIP

British Library Cataloguing-in-Publication data are available from
the British Library.

Contents

The Current Definition of ADHD
The Symptoms of ADHD
  Inattention
  Impulsivity
  Hyperactivity
ADHD: More Than One Problem?
Onset of ADHD
Prevalence of ADHD
Associated Problems
  Behavior Problems
  Other Emotional Problems
Parent–Child and Other Interpersonal
    Problems
School Learning Problems
Will My Child Outgrow ADHD?
Conclusion

Inheritance
Brain Differences

About the Authors

David L. Wodrich, Ph.D., A.B.P.P., is Clinical Director of Child Psychology at Phoenix Children's Hospital's Neuroscience Center. He has participated in the multidisciplinary Attention Deficit Hyperactivity Disorder Clinic at Phoenix Children's Hospital since its inception in 1987. His interests in children with attention deficit hyperactivity disorder include diagnosis, objective monitoring of behavior changes associated with medication usage, educational programming, and social skills development.

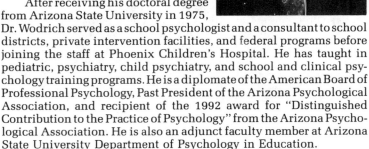

After receiving his doctoral degree from Arizona State University in 1975, Dr. Wodrich served as a school psychologist and a consultant to school districts, private intervention facilities, and federal programs before joining the staff at Phoenix Children's Hospital. He has taught in pediatric, psychiatry, child psychiatry, and school and clinical psychology training programs. He is a diplomate of the American Board of Professional Psychology, Past President of the Arizona Psychological Association, and recipient of the 1992 award for "Distinguished Contribution to the Practice of Psychology" from the Arizona Psychological Association. He is also an adjunct faculty member at Arizona State University Department of Psychology in Education.

The author of more than 25 papers, articles, chapters, and books, Dr. Wodrich's current interest is the effects of brain injury and dysfunction on children's learning. He lives with his wife, Susan, and children, Matt and Jill, in Mesa, Arizona.

CONTRIBUTORS

Robert R. Davila, Ph.D., served as Assistant Secretary for the Office of Special Education and Rehabilitative Services, U.S. Department of Education, during the administration of former President George Bush. During his term, he worked closely with the Assistant Secretaries for Elementary and Secondary Education and Civil Rights to clarify the question of eligibility for services for children with attention deficit disorders under Section 504 of the Rehabilitation Act and Part B of the Individuals with Disabilities Education Act (IDEA). Other priorities during his administration included increased funding to investigate and develop best practice models for the integration of children with disabilities into regular school programs, parent and family education, empowerment of persons with disabilities, involvement of external constituencies in providing input and direction to funding and program priorities, and improved monitoring of compliance with federal laws.

Dr. Davila, who is deaf, is a long-time educator of the deaf with teaching experience at all levels—elementary, secondary, undergraduate, and graduate. After receiving his Ph.D. from Syracuse University, he taught at and later served as Vice President for Precollege Programs at Gallaudet University. Following his government service, Dr. Davila was appointed Headmaster of the New York School for the Deaf at White Plains, the school where he began his professional career as a secondary-level mathematics teacher. He is the recipient of several honorary degrees and numerous awards for his contributions to the education of all Americans. He and his wife Donna are parents of two adult sons.

Martin Irwin, M.D., is the Director of the Division of Child and Adolescent Psychiatry and an Associate Professor of Psychiatry and Pediatrics at the State University of New York Health Science Center, Syracuse. He is a graduate of Cornell University and the University of Pennsylvania School of Medicine. After completing his training in psychiatry and in child psychiatry at the University of Chicago, he served on the medical faculties at Northwestern University, Tulane University, and Brown University. He is the author of *Psychiatric Hospitalization of Children* (Charles C Thomas, 1982) and has contributed numerous articles to professional journals. His major areas of interests include pediatric psychopharmacology, the process of mother–infant attachment, and the delivery of comprehensive mental health services to children who have not traditionally had access to child psychiatric services.

Foreword

One of our best studied child psychiatric disorders, attention deficit hyperactivity disorder (ADHD), is a common and relatively consistent problem. Even though the earliest clinical description dates back to the 1900s, it has only been in the past 5 years or so that attention has been given to parents of children with the disorder. Dr. Wodrich's aim in this book is to provide current information on ADHD in a clear, concise fashion to help parents deal with the various manifestations of this problem and the impact it has on their family life, as well as on the child's interpersonal life at home and at school.

Dr. Wodrich presents basic facts about ADHD and dispels common myths; discusses the value of various types of diagnostic instruments including interviews, rating scales, and observations; reviews the variety of methods of intervention that have shown to be effective for children with this disorder such as behavior modification, medication, and school-based interventions; discusses ways to find financial help; and presents information on the various types of educational programs that might be useful for children with ADHD.

The emphasis on educational placement is very important as school is probably the best single place to begin intervention for children with ADHD. Dr. Wodrich gives parents the information they need in order to become active members of the decision-making team and to work with teachers and other professionals to develop an intervention plan that works best for their child and family.

This book does more than simply review current thinking; it provides parents with the support necessary when living with a child with ADHD. For all parents facing the common problem of ADHD, this book is an essential resource.

Dennis P. Cantwell, M.D.
Joseph Campbell Professor
of Child Psychiatry
University of California,
Los Angeles

Preface

Most parents thirst for knowledge that can help their children. When it is suspected (or perhaps confirmed) that attention deficit hyperactivity disorder (ADHD) is present, parents quite naturally wish to have questions answered. In my experience with families at Phoenix Children's Hospital, three broad questions arise most often: What is attention deficit hyperactivity disorder and what causes it? How is it diagnosed? How is it treated? This book attempts to answer these questions.

My co-authors and I have tried to address parents' concerns directly. We have attempted to speak forthrightly, clearly, and honestly, as if you, a parent, were meeting face-to-face with us. Of course, the written format permits us to speak with a degree of detail impossible during a brief office visit. In addition, a book has other obvious advantages over a visit to a professional's office. Important sections of a book can be reread while less important sections for any particular family can be skimmed or skipped altogether.

For example, if your son or daughter is suspected of having attention deficit hyperactivity disorder but has yet to be evaluated by a professional, then Chapters 3–7 (within the section entitled, "How Is ADHD Diagnosed?") may be particularly worthwhile. In contrast, parents of a previously diagnosed child may find Chapters 8–15 (within the section entitled "How Is ADHD Treated?") most valuable. Focusing even more narrowly, a parent concerned about special education services for his or her child may turn directly to Chapter 10 ("ADHD and Eligibility for Special School Services"). Those concerned about medication may make Chapter 9 their first priority ("Medication Treatment in ADHD").

Although written with parents in mind, the book may also address concerns of teachers. Parents often request that information be shared with their son's or daughter's teacher(s). Generally, much of the information that parents find useful in understanding and living with their child proves valuable for classroom teachers too. Teachers who are seeking information about this condition may thus benefit from reading any or all of this book, although Chapters 10–12, which deal directly with educational issues, will probably be most useful. It would certainly be appropriate for parents who have found helpful information in this book to pass it along to their child's teacher. The book may also be a valuable supplement for teachers in training because it contains classroom suggestions. Also reviewed are eligibility requirements for special school services with input from Robert Davila, former Assistant Secretary for the Office of Special Education and Rehabilitative Services, U.S. Department of Education, during the administration of former President Bush.

While we trust that the book is valuable for parents, by its very nature it has limitations. First, the information provided is general. Direct application for your individual child should not necessarily be assumed. Nonetheless, the information in this book may constitute an initial knowledge base that will enable you to work more effectively with your child's professional caregivers, be they physicians, psychologists, or educators. You are strongly encouraged to identify a qualified professional who can perform a detailed evaluation and assist you in all aspects of intervention. With regard to issues of medication, of course, it is essential that you work under the direction of your child's physician. Only he or she knows your child's health status and history well enough to render care appropriately. Second, this volume is intended for parents. It is not a scholarly treatise on attention deficit hyperactivity disorder such as practicing professionals or students in psychology or medicine might require. Those seeking more in-depth and critical information are referred to excellent sources such as *Attention Deficit Hyperactivity Disorder: A Handbook for Diagnosis and Treatment* (1990), by Russell Barkley.

I would also like to point out that the case examples contained in this volume are fictitious as to the precise details presented. They are invented examples designed to depict important points. While details are contrived, the general points reflect essential information gained from working with many children and families.

Finally, with regard to the format of this book, I have elected to include all reference citations at the end of the text in order to be less disruptive for the reader. It is hoped that this consolidation augments the usefulness and enhances the accessibility of this volume for professional and lay readers alike.

I have been fortunate to work with many excellent colleagues at Phoenix Children's Hospital. Three of my medical colleagues, pediatric neurologist Dr. Saunder Bernes and child psychiatrists Dr. Eric Benjamin and Dr. Randall Ricardi, reviewed chapters for accuracy and clarity. I wish to thank them for their kind assistance.

Finally, I would like to thank my wife and children for their understanding and indulgence while I monopolized our home computer over the many months of manuscript preparation. You guys can have it back, but I make no promises about the future!

Attention Deficit Hyperactivity Disorder

WHAT IS ADHD AND WHAT CAUSES IT?

Chapter 1

Definition and Characteristics of ADHD

E xactly what is attention deficit hyperactivity disorder (ADHD)? If your child has been diagnosed as having ADHD or you suspect that he or she demonstrates symptoms of the disorder, the answer to this question is crucial. Given an understanding of the disorder's characteristics, a plan to help your child can be devised. Without this understanding, you and your child will likely experience unnecessary frustration. If you are unsure whether your child is affected by ADHD, familiarizing yourself with its definition and characteristics may help you to decide to either seek professional diagnostic assistance or conclude that your child does not have ADHD.

THE CURRENT DEFINITION OF ADHD

Attention deficit hyperactivity disorder lacks a single, universally accepted definition. In fact, the term itself was coined in 1987 (for a discussion regarding the changing terminology of ADHD, see Illustration 1.1).

THE PAST

Minimal Brain Dysfunction

Among the early labels used to describe children now referred to as having attention deficit hyperactivity disorder was minimal brain dysfunction. An epidemic of encephalitis (inflammation of the brain) early in this century left many with problems of inattention, impulsivity, and hyperactivity. Thereafter, these deficits were thought to be neurological problems, since they were seen as clear consequences of brain injury among epidemic survivors. When the same set of deficits (inattention, impulsivity, hyperactivity) was noted among children without known brain injury, it was assumed that some unidentified brain injury must be present, but that it must be extremely subtle, hard to detect, or "minimal." This minimal brain injury, or minimal brain dysfunction, was believed to be the root of all inattention, impulsivity, and hyperactivity problems for which no clear history of brain injury existed. As a result, hyperactive or inattentive children were often referred to as having minimal brain damage or dysfunction. This label continued through the 1950s and 1960s.

Hyperkinetic Reaction of Childhood

With publication of the *Diagnostic and Statistical Manual* (2nd ed., DSM-II) in 1968, reference was made to children with these deficits, but "hyperactivity" was singled out as the predominant element. DSM-II thus included "Hyperkinetic [meaning hyper motoric movement] Reaction of Childhood" among its childhood disorders. During the 1960s and 1970s children with ADHD were often referred to as "hyperkinetic," or more simply, "hyperactive."

Illustration 1.1. ADHD: Past and future terminology of the disorder

An important source for understanding ADHD is a lengthy volume published by the American Psychiatric Association in 1987 titled *Diagnostic and Statistical Manual of Mental Disorders* (3rd ed., rev.).[1] This volume—a standard and authoritative source for U.S. practitioners, researchers, and others in the field of

---

[1]For ease of reading, specific reference citations do not appear in the text. The interested reader should refer to the reference list at the end of this book.

Attention Deficit Disorder (ADD) with Hyperactivity and *Attention Deficit Disorder (ADD) without Hyperactivity*

With DSM-III, published in 1980, attention deficit disorder (ADD) became the new title because some researchers had come to believe that inattention was the central deficiency. Symptoms for ADD were listed under three broad clusters: inattention, impulsivity, and hyperactivity. It should be noted that at that time it was possible to assign either a diagnosis of attention deficit disorder with hyperactivity *or* attention deficit disorder without hyperactivity, depending on whether or not hyperactivity accompanied inattention and impulsivity. People today who still use the acronym ADD rather than ADHD are simply using the old terminology.

THE FUTURE

Will the term *attention deficit hyperactivity disorder* be replaced? Although a definitive answer cannot be given at present, the answer will ultimately come with the publication of DSM-IV. Available information as this book goes to press suggests that the currently used 14-item symptom list outlined in DSM-III-R is likely to be replaced in light of recent empirical studies. In DSM-IV, symptoms will be grouped under the heading of either "Inattention" or "Hyperactivity/Impulsivity." Individuals with symptoms primarily in the first category would be designated as ADHD "predominately inattentive type," whereas those with symptoms primarily in the second category would be considered ADHD "predominately hyperactive–impulsive type." Those with significant symptoms in both categories would thus be ADHD "combined type."

mental disorders—is commonly referred to by its abbreviation, DSM-III-R. An updated version of this manual (DSM-IV) is due to be published in December 1993 (please do not be put off by these acronyms; they are not used excessively in this book). DSM-III-R contains formal definitions for virtually every conceivable emotional, learning, or behavior problem ranging from reading disorders to severe depression. It is the source from which the definition of ADHD is derived for use in this book.

Table 1.1 outlines the criteria for defining ADHD.

Table 1.1. DSM-III-R criteria for attention deficit hyperactivity disorder

A. A disturbance of at least six months during which at least eight of the following are present:

    (1)   often fidgets with hands or feet or squirms in seat (in adolescents, may be limited to subjective feelings of restlessness)

    (2)   has difficulty remaining seated when required to do so

    (3)   is easily distracted by extraneous stimuli

    (4)   has difficulty awaiting turn in games or group situations

    (5)   often blurts out answers to questions before they have been completed

    (6)   has difficulty following through on instructions from others (not due to oppositional behavior or failure of comprehension), e.g., fails to finish chores

    (7)   has difficulty sustaining attention in tasks or play activities

    (8)   often shifts from one uncompleted activity to another

    (9)   has difficulty playing quietly

    (10) often talks excessively

    (11) often interrupts or intrudes on others, e.g., butts into other children's games

    (12) often does not seem to listen to what is being said to him or her

    (13) often loses things necessary for tasks or activities at school or at home (e.g., toys, pencils, books, assignments)

    (14) often engages in physically dangerous activities without considering possible consequences (not for the purpose of thrill-seeking), e.g., runs into street without looking

B. Onset before the age of seven.

C. Does not meet the criteria for a Pervasive Developmental Disorder.

From American Psychiatric Association. (1987). *Diagnostic and statistical manual of mental disorders* (3rd ed., rev.) (pp. 52–53). Washington, DC: American Psychiatric Association; reprinted by permission.

You are encouraged to study these criteria closely in determining whether your child may have ADHD. Three conditions must be met in diagnosing ADHD: 1) presence of at least eight symptoms listed in Table 1.1, 2) presence of symptoms for 6 months or longer, and 3) presence of symptoms before 7 years of age. It is additionally assumed that no other DSM-III-R disorder accounts for these symptoms as readily as ADHD. A child is diagnosed as having ADHD only after data have been compiled from several sources such as observations, interviews, and rating forms. The focus of this chapter, however, is understanding precisely what these symptoms mean.

THE SYMPTOMS OF ADHD

It is difficult for most parents to remember each of the symptoms outlined in Table 1.1, much less comprehend precisely what each encompasses. To better understand the nature of ADHD, you are encouraged to simplify your thinking. Three deficits have long been identified as typically underlying these symptoms, and understanding them first is easier than tackling the whole list. The three deficits are: inattention, impulsivity, and hyperactivity. By examining the DSM-III-R symptoms in Table 1.1, you may appreciate how these primary deficits cause problems.

Inattention

Inattention refers to errors either in selecting what to attend to or in keeping attention focused for as long as necessary to perform a task. Two of the symptoms from the DSM-III-R list that are tied to attention problems are: "is easily distracted by extraneous stimuli" (#3, Table 1.1) and "has difficulty sustaining attention in tasks or play activities" (#7, Table 1.1). These symptoms can be readily recognized by parents. What is surprising to parents, however, is that children with ADHD are extremely variable in exhibiting their attention problems. On the one hand, a child with ADHD may have no problem concentrating on highly stimulating activities or ones that the child selects for himself or herself. A child with even fairly severe ADHD may show no difficulties in these situations. On the other hand, he or she may appear distractible, inattentive, or may give up quickly when confronted with repetitive or tedious tasks. Thus, an 8-year-old boy with ADHD may work for hours without interruption while playing a video game, but may sustain attention for only a few minutes during monotonous arithmetic drills at school. A 5-year-old girl with ADHD may organize and reorganize dolls provided that playmates are present, but may wander from activity to activity during solitary play. In other words, the demands of the situation may determine the severity of symptoms that are evident.

The pervasiveness of these problems across situations and their chronicity is the key to deciding if your child is genuinely inattentive. It isn't fair to evaluate only the best or worst instances of inattention. However, if adult direction, close supervision, high levels of rewards, or high-interest activities are required to sustain attention, then a bona fide problem may exist. In the final analysis, someone must make a judgment about whether or not each of the individual symptoms related to inattention is present. Again, as is emphasized in Chapters 3–7, multiple data sources can aid this process.

Impulsivity

Impulsivity means that the individual has difficulty properly controlling or regulating impulses. The urge to act is expressed too readily in behavior; the typical controls that are expected of a child of a given age simply fail. Symptoms that appear to be tied to impulsivity are: "has difficulty awaiting turn in games or group situations" (#4, Table 1.1); "has difficulty playing quietly" (#9, Table 1.1); and "often talks excessively" (#10, Table 1.1). As an example, a child with ADHD may undercontrol his or her impulses during a simple board game. The exuberance to make a quick deal, to roll the dice, or to comment on others' play is often expressed unchecked. This makes the child apt to play out of turn, to grab the dice before another player has finished, or to make too many careless or inappropriate comments about the play of others.

Social difficulties seem to spring from impulse control deficits. Impulsive behavior is apt to annoy other children. It can also frustrate parents. Virtually any situation involving rules or expectations can result in adult/child conflict. For example, children with ADHD often fail to recognize obligatory classroom behavior such as keeping hands to self, talking quietly, or remaining quiet and seated. The child with ADHD may require constant reminders, reprimands, and redirection to control impulses. Teachers and parents often complain of exhaustion after caring for a child with ADHD. Because the child's internal controls of behavior are so deficient, parents complain that they must constantly restate expectations and enforce rules with yelling or threats of heavy-handed punishment. Note: Chapter 8 shares ways in which parents can most effectively manage the behavior of a child with ADHD.

Hyperactivity

Hyperactivity relates to excesses in physical movement, especially excesses that have a purposeless, poorly directed, or driven quality. Symptoms related to hyperactivity are: "often fidgets with hands or feet or squirms in seat" (#1, Table 1.1); and "has difficulty remaining seated when required to do so" (#2, Table 1.1). Children with ADHD are more restless, fidgety, and on-the-go than children without ADHD. Situations requiring quiet, focused, and controlled behavior seem to present special problems for children with ADHD, whereas more open settings may be no problem. This is because a child who races about the playground may trouble no one, but teacher and peers find it troublesome when a boy gets up repeatedly to sharpen an already-sharp pencil, or a girl persists in leaving her bus seat to visit with friends despite warnings from the driver, or a teenager cannot sit through an entire movie without multiple trips to the snackbar or restroom. With the hyperactivity dimension, too, a judgment must be made about the appropriateness of the behavior for the situation and age of the child. The requirement of judgment makes diagnosis of ADHD less simple than it appears on the surface. Later chapters describe how the information necessary for an ADHD diagnosis is collected.

ADHD: MORE THAN ONE PROBLEM?

As the previous discussion of deficits implies, ADHD may be several interrelated problems, rather than a single problem. In fact, analysis of parent and teacher questionnaires completed on hundreds of children has led researchers to conclude that ADHD is not a single condition that appears equivalently in all individuals. Rather, two main underlying deficits seem present among the many individuals studied: inattention and hyperactivity. Impulsivity shows up less distinctively in these empirical studies. Some researchers have argued that inattention and hyperactivity are the central aspects of ADHD.

It is important to point out, however, that *both* inattention and hyperactivity may not be present in all children with ADHD. It appears that some children have predominantly attentional deficits but no hyperactivity, whereas others have both attentional and hyperactivity deficits. These children seem to differ from each other in important ways. Inattentive and hyperactive children, for instance, are apt to have more social difficulties and a harder time following rules. By contrast, inattentive children who are not hyperactive may be more anxious and shy. Recent research has also suggested that these children may respond somewhat differently to the most frequently used type of medication, the stimulants. Table 1.2 lists characteristics that seem to distinguish these two groups of children.

Prior to the publication of DSM-III-R in 1987, clinicians easily diagnosed children who were inattentive but not hyperactive. They were summarily diagnosed as having "attention deficit disorder without hyperactivity." Conversely, children who exhibited inattention and hyperactivity were diagnosed as having "attention

Table 1.2. Differences among children with attentional problems with and without hyperactivity

With hyperactivity	Without hyperactivity
Conduct problems	Sluggish, drowsy
Impulsive	Daydreaming
Distractible	Anxious, shy
Rejected by peers	Learning disabilities
Higher-dose stimulants	Lower-dose stimulants

Note: The differences listed are generally true. Individual children, however, may or may not show any or all of these differences.

deficit disorder *with* hyperactivity." DSM-III-R, which is still the most current volume in the field, does not offer an easy method for diagnosing an attention problem without hyperactivity. As this book is going to press, it appears that DSM-IV will identify three subgroupings of "attention deficit/hyperactivity disorder:" a "predominately inattentive type," a "predominately hyperactive type," and a "combined type" that exhibits symptoms of both previous subgroupings. In other words, clinicians will again have an easy way to diagnose a child as having attention problems but not hyperactivity. To some extent, the distinctive nature of children with attentional but not hyperactivity problems has continued to be recognized despite the fact that DSM-III-R has shown little concern with making the distinction. You may notice case examples in this book regarding children who are inattentive but not hyperactive. Regardless of any changes in definitions, terminology, or criteria in DSM-IV, the principles discussed herein will remain applicable.

ONSET OF ADHD

The DSM-III-R definition of ADHD requires that symptoms appear before the child is 7 years of age and be present for a 6-month duration before a diagnosis can be made. This requirement is seldom a problem. In fact, the average age that symptoms first become evident has been found to be 3–4 years of age. Many parents report that their child was hyperactive, restless, driven, and constantly on the go since he or she was a toddler, or even before. Others recall brief attention, lack of inhibition in social situations, and poor appreciation of danger among their 2- or 3-year-olds. Some researchers have even suggested that babies differ on the characteristics of attention span and activity level.

Although many children are recognized as having ADHD when they are preschoolers, many are not. Not surprisingly, school is the challenge for many children that causes their inattention, overactivity, or self-control deficits to become manifest in behavior. For these children, the demand to cope with a new situation means that a previously underlying but undetected deficit now is unmistakably present in day-to-day behavior. Some parents are confused that a child who seemed fine as a preschooler suddenly has ADHD as a kindergartner. It is usually true that the deficit did not emerge for the first time at age 5 (upon beginning kindergarten); rather, the school requirements of, for example, lining up quietly, refraining from talking, and sticking on task culminated in symptoms unmistakable to a classroom teacher.

PREVALENCE OF ADHD

It is estimated that 1%–12% of school-age children are affected by ADHD, with 3% the consensus estimate. Precise estimates of the percentage of affected children are virtually impossible because of the changing definition of the disorder. Definitions in DSM-III-R were formulated by a committee of experts who were obliged to set standards, which are often arbitrary. For example, the current definition calls for 8 out of 14 symptoms to be present. If the committee had selected a 10-symptom cutoff, then fewer children would be identifiable; if they had selected a 6-symptom cutoff, more would be identifiable. Chapter 6 points out that rating instruments allow researchers and clinicians to remove some of the imprecision of diagnosing ADHD.

In whatever way ADHD is defined, it is clear that far more boys than girls are affected, by ratios estimated at from 2 to 1 to 10 to 1. Why this maldistribution? Many researchers believe that a greater inherent risk, perhaps related to brain biochemistry or structure, exists for males. Others have pointed to the school-related demand to sit quietly and attend. These demands may be relatively harder for males because of the manner in which they are socialized. Still others have wondered about subtle discrimination occurring among elementary teachers, who are predominantly female. No clear answer is available.

ASSOCIATED PROBLEMS

A major advance in recent research has revealed a number of problems that can accompany ADHD. Children, teenagers, and even adults are at risk for a variety of these associated problems. Although ADHD's symptoms can be troubling in their own right for parents, teachers, peers, and the individuals themselves, often coexisting problems with behavior control, school learning, and social relations can be even more disturbing. Many parents, and a surprising number of professionals, mistakenly assume that ADHD is a harmless disorder characterized by too much busy activity but few other negatives. This assumption is wrong, as careful studies have shown.

Behavior Problems

Figure 1.1 depicts ADHD as one of three disruptive behavior disorders, as categorized by DSM-III-R. The three disorders in this category, ADHD, conduct disorder, and oppositional defiant disorder, occur together frequently, although the disorders also frequently exist alone, without the presence of the others. In many instances, these are not benign disorders. Each is often

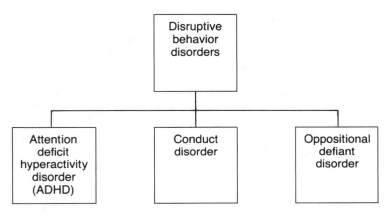

Figure 1.1. DSM-III-R categorization of ADHD as disruptive behavior disorders (see text for description).

socially disruptive or distressing, and each can have a significant negative impact on the child's life. Since it is important for you as a parent to understand ADHD's relationship to these other disorders, brief descriptions of conduct disorder and oppositional defiant disorder are included next.

Conduct disorder, as described by DSM-III-R, is "a persistent pattern of conduct in which the basic rights of others and major age-appropriate societal norms or rules are violated" (p. 53). Table 1.3 contains a complete set of diagnostic criteria for conduct disorder. Briefly, the symptoms relate to breaking rules and participating in antisocial behavior, such as stealing, running away from home, lying, and truancy. Recent estimates suggest that 30%–50% of children with ADHD between the ages of 7 and 10 years are likely to show antisocial symptoms and symptoms of conduct disorder. These symptoms may bring children with ADHD into conflict with authority and lead to severe prob-

Table 1.3. DSM-III-R conduct disorder criteria

A. A disturbance of conduct lasting at least six months, during which at least three of the following have been present:

   (1) has stolen without confrontation of a victim on more than one occasion (including forgery)

   (2) has run away from home overnight at least twice while living in parental or parental surrogate home (or once without returning)

   (3) often lies (other than to avoid physical or sexual abuse)

   (4) has deliberately engaged in fire-setting

   (5) is often truant from school (for older person, absent from work)

   (6) has broken into someone else's house, building, or car

   (7) has deliberately destroyed others' property (other than by fire-setting)

   (8) has been physically cruel to animals

   (9) has forced someone into sexual activity with him or her

   (10) has used a weapon in more than one fight

   (11) often initiates physical fights

   (12) has stolen with confrontation of a victim (e.g., mugging, purse-snatching, extortion, armed robbery)

   (13) has been physically cruel to people

From American Psychiatric Association. (1987). *Diagnostic and statistical manual of mental disorders* (3rd ed., rev.) (p. 55). Washington, DC: American Psychiatric Association; reprinted by permission.

lems unless they are corrected by the late teenage or adult years.

Oppositional defiant disorder is defined by DSM-III-R as "a pattern of negativistic, hostile, and defiant behavior without the more serious violations of basic rights of others that are seen in Conduct Disorder" (p. 56). The complete criteria for this disorder are listed in Table 1.4. The symptoms cover excesses of behaviors such as temper outbursts, arguing with and defying adults, blaming others, and responding vindictively. Although encompassing symptoms less severe than

Table 1.4. DSM-III-R oppositional defiant disorder criteria

A. A disturbance of at least six months during which at least five of the following are present:

   (1) often loses temper

   (2) often argues with adults

   (3) often actively defies or refuses adult requests or rules, e.g., refuses to do chores at home

   (4) often deliberately does things that annoy people, e.g., grabs other children's hats

   (5) often blames others for his or her own mistakes

   (6) is often touchy or easily annoyed by others

   (7) is often angry and resentful

   (8) is often spiteful or vindictive

   (9) often swears or uses obscene language

B. Does not meet the criteria for Conduct Disorder, and does not occur exclusively during the course of a psychotic disorder, Dysthymia, or a Major Depressive, Hypomanic, or Manic Episode.

From American Psychiatric Association. (1987). *Diagnostic and statistical manual of mental disorders* (3rd ed., rev.) (pp. 57–58). Washington, DC: American Psychiatric Association; reprinted by permission.

conduct disorder, oppositional defiant disorder embraces behaviors that can, nonetheless, produce severe strains at home and at school, although some children are much less symptomatic outside their own homes. In a recent study at the University of Massachusetts Medical Center, Russell Barkley and colleagues found that when rating forms were used to identify the most ADHD-symptomatic 3% of a group of children, 59% of those children also met the criteria for oppositional defiant disorder. This is an enormous overlap; it implies, as have other studies, that approximately half the children with ADHD also have severe problems with compliance, temper control, and cooperation. As shown in Chapters 3–7, a thorough evaluation does not stop once a diagnosis of ADHD has been established; a full accounting of the child's problems (including possible conduct or oppositional aspects), and strengths, must be accomplished.

Why do conduct and oppositional disorders and attentional and impulse disorders occur together so often? Several answers have been postulated. It may be that the deficits associated with ADHD, such as poor regulation of impulses and problems sustaining attention, prime the child for behavior problems. If this is so, it is easy to see how arguing, losing one's temper, or even stealing may be a consequence of deficient impulse control or of poor attention to rewards and punishments. Another explanation suggests a single common cause for ADHD, oppositional defiant disorder, and conduct disorder. Whatever malfunction exists in the child's nervous system, or in his or her personal history, causes multiple problems to eventuate, ADHD being just one of them and behavior and conduct problems being others. Feelings of frustration and anger resulting from chronic failure may also be implicated. Children with ADHD often feel as though they can do little right. After failing at school or receiving repeated negative parental and peer feedback, anger accrues. Too often it may boil over into unacceptable conduct. Likewise, the child with ADHD who has experienced little success in socially accepted endeavors, such as school, clubs, or family, may turn elsewhere in search of success. Success sometimes occurs only in unacceptable, antisocial activities. When this happens repeatedly, a pattern of breaking rules and affiliating with other children or teenagers who do the same may occur, and conduct disorder may ensue. As a parent, it is important for you to recognize the risk for these types of problems without forgetting that they occur only among *some* children with ADHD.

Other Emotional Problems

Given all the negatives that happen to them, children with ADHD are, not surprisingly, more subject to poor self-esteem than typical children. As adults, they have more depression-related problems, such as severe discouragement and demoralization. Yet, clear evidence is lacking that children with ADHD are more likely than children without ADHD to have severe depression.

Two other DSM-III-R conditions, tic disorder and Tourette's syndrome, occur more often among children with ADHD, albeit only in a small minority. Tics are repetitive twitches or movements, usually around the eye or face but sometimes involving vocal noises. Tourette's syndrome involves both motor and vocal tics that extend over a long time (greater than 1 year). Although many tics are mild and may be virtually unnoticeable to the untrained observer, some tics are severe and chronic. The rarer Tourette's syndrome may involve other problems, such as self-injurious behavior or an irresistible urge to swear. Many times parents, and even treating professionals, overlook the presence of tics. Often the repetitive motor tics are written off as mere "nervous habits," while vocal tics are often thought to be throat clearing or sniffing as a result of allergies. One reason it is important to recognize tics is that their presence may suggest that some medications would be inappropriate for use with this child (see Chapter 9).

PARENT–CHILD AND OTHER INTERPERSONAL PROBLEMS

Among the many things parents must teach children are: to follow rules, to dress and groom themselves, to complete homework, and to cooperate. Impaired by difficulty attending and by poor impulse modulation, the child with ADHD is bound to struggle with these tasks. All too often, the parent–child relationship is strained as a result. Many parents find they must repeat directions, use immediate, potent, and frequent consequences, or constantly organize their child's life. If they don't do these things, they have tenuous control over their child's behavior or their child seems to fail constantly. It is little wonder that parental frustration and fatigue develop. Perhaps it is because of these factors that much more self-blame and depression is found among mothers of children with ADHD. These same factors may cause stresses throughout the family; parents of children with ADHD are three times more likely to divorce than are parents of unaffected children.

Parents of children with ADHD have been shown by research to use more commands to direct their children and to be more negative toward them. Such parents often comment that without loud commands or threats of punishment, there would be little cooperation. Not surprisingly, families often find that one of the most valuable services professionals can offer is to teach alternative methods to govern these difficult-to-discipline children. (For a detailed discussion, see Chapter 8.)

For some children with ADHD, winning and maintaining friends is a special challenge. The core deficits of inattention, impulsivity, and hyperactivity once again prevent success, this time in the social realm. If other 7-year-olds regularly spend 40 minutes sitting attentively and organizing their baseball cards, the 7-year-old with ADHD whose attention for this activity is 5 minutes may fail to fit in. Similarly, if the social expectation is to speak quietly at a party and contribute to but not dominate a conversation, the 14-year-old who impulsively interrupts to speak loudly and incessantly about himself is apt to be rejected. So too is the child who plays too actively, roughly, and with such exuberance as to imperil playmates' safety. It is for these reasons that children with ADHD are often rated as unpopular (i.e., nonpreferred as playmates) in research studies. It is also why children with ADHD often try to find a niche with children far younger or far older than themselves.

SCHOOL LEARNING PROBLEMS

A strong association exists between ADHD and school problems. The ADHD symptom list (Table 1.1) itself seems to revolve around problems with school origins. After all, it is in the classroom where one is expected to remain seated, refrain from answering until the question is completed, and see a task through to completion.

Children with ADHD may experience several types of trouble at school. First, they may be underproductive— that is, fail to complete assignments or lose their work— or be disorganized. Therefore, they may risk failure because work is not done. Parents may be told their child can't be awarded passing grades even though he or she seems knowledgeable about the subjects taught because not enough work is being completed.

Second, children with ADHD may have learning disabilities. Disorders of memory, language, visual perception, or the like that are severe enough to prevent the child from achieving up to potential are more common among children with ADHD. Unlike the underproductive child who knows how to read but fails to complete his worksheets, the child with learning disabilities has not learned to read (or do mathematics, or spelling, or other academics). It is estimated that approximately 3% of children in the United States without ADHD are afflicted with learning disabilities. Among children with ADHD, the percentage jumps to as high as 35%, by some estimates. Learning disabilities are particularly devastating for children with ADHD, because they struggle to learn and to produce work in class.

Third, behavior and conduct problems may be evident at school, just as they may be at home. Unfortunately, the typical public school classroom has too many students and too little teacher time to allow easy individualization of instruction and discipline. Many children with ADHD are expelled from school or are labeled as severe discipline problems, often without appreciation that they are affected with a disorder that contributes to their behavior. Other children with ADHD merit and receive special school services (related either to their behavior/emotional status or to their learning disabilities). Chapters 10–12 provide information about how children with ADHD may be helped in school.

WILL MY CHILD OUTGROW ADHD?

"It's too bad my son has this hyperactivity problem, but he *will* outgrow it, won't he?" Many parents have heard that ADHD is confined to the childhood years; they expect the disorder to disappear by the teenage years and certainly by adulthood. The answer to this concerned parent's question is yes and no.

If 100 8-year-olds highly symptomatic with ADHD were followed until they reached 16 years of age, certainly fewer than 100 of them would still be found to be symptomatic. Those who were would probably behave much differently than they did as 8-year-olds. Most would have slowed motorically, would attend better to repetitive tasks, and would regulate their impulses better. Physiologic maturation and the myriad of learning experiences encountered in growing up would guarantee this outcome.

Sadly, approximately 75 out of the group would continue to have problems at school, with their families, or with authorities. Although their behavior may appear more mature than it did when they were 8 years old, the same underlying deficits may remain. For example, impulsivity now may interfere with responsible completion of chores or homework, or with following community rules such as curfew. As teens, the ADHD group may exercise poor judgment when they are unsupervised and with peers. One-quarter or more might exhibit antisocial or conduct disordered behavior (e.g., stealing, running away, or truancy). Almost 60 would be anticipated to have failed one grade in school. Thus, although as teenagers many of these children would appear less conspicuously inattentive or hyperactive, many nonetheless would continue to struggle in life.

Several factors seem to lessen the risk of teen problems: high IQ, high social status of the family, good peer relations, few aggressive and conduct problems as children, parents without emotional problems, and a relatively problem-free history of interactions with parents. The more of these factors that are present in the child's favor, the better the chances of good long-term adjustment.

If we followed the same set of individuals even further forward in time, a surprising prevalence of problems would yet be found. As adults, as many as 50%–65% would still be symptomatic for ADHD. As many as 25% might have actual antisocial personalities as adults—with accompanying problems (court involvement, most often for problems such as traffic violations), physical aggression toward others, and theft. This group of adults would also be expected to change jobs more frequently, to work less well independently, and to be less likely to get along well with their supervisors. Although clear evidence of greater prevalence of mood disorders is lacking, rates of attempted and successfully completed suicides among adults who had ADHD as children is higher than among adults without this history. This fact may be due to years of frustration and discouragement.

CONCLUSION

ADHD represents a set of interrelated deficiencies with attention, activity level, and impulse control that often results in educational, social, parent–child, and vocational problems, some of which continue into adulthood. As demonstrated in subsequent chapters, comprehensive assessment and intervention are essential for maximizing the individual's adjustment and promoting long-term happiness.

Chapter 2

Causes of ADHD

Scientists and parents share an equal interest in locating the causes of ADHD—scientists because they want to find better ways to treat or prevent ADHD, and parents because, while they also seek modes of treatment or prevention, are eager, too, for an answer to their personal dilemma of "why my child?" Considerable research has been devoted to the search for causes. Although a precise understanding of ADHD's cause remains elusive, a general understanding of the origins of the disorder has emerged. In addition, we now know much more about what does *not* cause ADHD. Such findings have allowed several myths about ADHD's causes to be dispelled.

INHERITANCE

The current scientific consensus is that ADHD is principally an inherited condition. This is known by studying the characteristics of biologic relatives of individuals with ADHD. Using this strategy, Dennis Cantwell at the University of California at Los Angeles observed in 1972 that children with ADHD were far more likely to have relatives, especially fathers and uncles, with ADHD than were children without ADHD. More recently, it was found that between 20% and 32% of children with ADHD also have a parent or sibling with ADHD. Clearly, for many individuals, a genetic factor must cause or at least contribute to the emergence of ADHD. Several additional studies have examined families of children with ADHD, not only for the disorder itself but for associated problems. These studies have generally found that ADHD is associated with family members who have histories of aggression, legal difficulties, and mood problems. Speculation that a common underlying deficit may be present in the brain's operation or biochemistry has subsequently arisen. Of course, since biologic relatives also may share a common environment (i.e., live in the same household), learned behavior, in addition to inherited characteristics, may contribute to the family-related patterns of symptoms.

Some small-scale but interesting studies have addressed this latter point. Identical twins (genetically the same) and fraternal twins (genetically no more alike than siblings) have been closely examined. One study determined that when the identical-twin siblings of four children with ADHD were assessed, all of them also had ADHD. But when fraternal-twin siblings of children with ADHD were examined, only about 17% had ADHD. Subsequent studies, some using much larger numbers of twins, have produced findings that continue to show much greater co-occurrence of ADHD when twins are genetically identical. Since identical and fraternal twins share the same social environment and differ only in their genetic similarity, scientists are offered a unique chance to study the effects of inheritance. The strikingly greater similarity of identical over fraternal twins must be due to their common genes.

Experts who have examined all of the inheritance studies have offered conclusions. Current research shows that ADHD can be understood as between 30% to 50% inherited, with the child's social environment playing a much smaller causative role. Current knowledge is insufficient to explain a large portion of the causes of ADHD. Moreover, although inheritance explains much, a great deal remains to be discovered about precisely how inheritance works. Why some individuals are affected and others are not, or why males are more affected than females, is not entirely clear.

In the real world of the individual child with ADHD, many family patterns may be found: some individuals with ADHD have ADHD-diagnosed relatives, some have ADHD-suspected relatives, and some have entirely ADHD-free relatives. Even for the child with ADHD who has no relatives with ADHD-related problems, the disorder may be inherited. Just as families composed of short- or average-stature individuals occasionally produce a very tall child, so too may the family with no ADHD produce a child who is symptomatic for ADHD.

BRAIN DIFFERENCES

Scientists are now seeking the brain site(s) and nature of the brain's imperfection that may underlie ADHD. Some of their findings have been reported in the popular press, such as an investigation by Zametkin and colleagues at the National Institutes of Health. Using a scanning technique called positron emission tomography (PET scan), which allows study of the brain's use of glucose, these researchers found differing use of glucose between individuals with a history of ADHD and those without such a history. More interesting, they found that areas of the brain involved in motor planning and control and those that control arousal and attention used less glucose or were underactive in individuals with a history of ADHD. Of further importance is that this study, by identifying a physical/biomedical difference in individuals with ADHD symptoms helps refute the claims of those who have contended that ADHD merely represents a nonphysical behavioral style, or that the disorder itself is a myth.

Although the Zametkin et al. study involved only a few subjects and its conclusions must be viewed tentatively, its findings agree with other exploratory studies. Other small-scale studies of people with ADHD have found decreased blood flow and less electrical activity in brain centers related to planning and control. Psychological tests designed to measure the performance of specific sites in the brain have also found that centers that subsume regulation of impulse suppression work poorly among individuals with ADHD. Additional studies have also found differing levels of chemicals involved in nerve transmission between ADHD and non-ADHD individuals. These crucial chemicals, called neurotransmitters, appear deficient in ADHD individuals in a portion of the brain believed related to rewards and punishment.

Collectively, these studies imply that deficient functioning in those areas of the brain that involve response inhibition, attention, and sensitivity to rewards and punishment may characterize at least some individuals with ADHD. This research offers hope for advancing treatment. Perhaps medication's action could be better understood if the actual brain deficits underlying ADHD were identified and their function in producing symptoms elucidated. At present, however, these findings have no direct impact on ADHD treatment. By the same token, the sophisticated laboratory techniques used in these studies currently have no clear role in the routine clinical assessment of individual children with ADHD (see Chapter 9).

BRAIN INJURY

As indicated in Chapter 1, earlier in this century many clinicians assumed that ADHD symptoms were manifestations of brain injury. Not surprisingly, the connection between ADHD and brain injury has been extensively researched.

Children with ADHD have had their histories scrutinized for evidence of brain injury, yet less than 5% of those studied had evidence of actual brain damage. That is, events such as head trauma, brain infection, and stroke simply failed to account for many cases of ADHD. Although brain injury is not a common cause of ADHD, it may indeed cause symptoms of hyperactivity, impulsivity, and inattention. For example, children who have sustained severe head traumas often manifest conspicuous ADHD symptoms, but generally as part of a multifaceted clinical picture. In instances of clear-cut brain injury, the child's physician typically recognizes the unique causative factors so that the child's condition is distinguished from the ADHD disorder described in this book.

Subtle, difficult-to-detect brain injury has also been extensively investigated, as well as possible birth-related brain injury. Events surrounding birth such as lack of oxygen, or prematurity, have shown only a weak association with later development of ADHD. Other factors that may affect the fetus before birth, such as maternal smoking or alcohol use, have also been investigated without clear evidence of a causative role in ADHD. Among those children who do have ADHD as a result of pregnancy or birth-related problems, other evidence of brain injury may also be present that can be detected by a health care professional.

GENETIC ANOMALIES

Rare genetic disorders can be associated with ADHD symptoms. Children with, for example, neurofibromatosis, Turner syndrome, or fragile X syndrome are known to experience high rates of ADHD. They usually have other obvious problems as well. For instance, children with neurofibromatosis have multiple skin lesions, and may experience other health problems; the disorder often runs in families—thus its manifestation is generally noted before the onset of ADHD symptoms. As another example, children with fragile X syndrome often have a variety of physical and learning problems in addition to ADHD symptoms. If your child has a complicated history that includes physical differences, delayed development, or behavioral peculiarities, then his or her ADHD symptoms may represent something other than the common ADHD discussed in this book. A thorough evaluation is obviously essential.

FOOD ADDITIVES, SUGAR, AND ENVIRONMENTAL TOXINS

Since Benjamin Feingold proposed food coloring and additives as possible causes of ADHD in 1973, the notion of environmental substances as a cause of ADHD has drawn wide attention. Articles in the popular press have claimed that dyes and preservatives can somehow alter the brain's chemical balance and induce ADHD symptoms. The apparent explosion in the occurrence of ADHD during this century is attributed by some to the increased use of such additives and dyes.

Concern has also been expressed about sugar. Since sugar (glucose) is the energy source used by the brain, there has been broad speculation that sugar ingestion could stimulate the brain, perhaps leading to hyperactive behavior. Many parents and teachers alike report symptom exacerbation when sugar loads increase.

Although intuitively plausible, several carefully controlled empirical studies have not found food additives and sugar to be a cause of ADHD. Moreover, despite Feingold's reports that an additive-free diet reduced ADHD symptoms, subsequent and more carefully controlled studies by independent researchers have failed to replicate these findings. At present, most experts conclude there is little reason to advocate an altered diet for most children with ADHD. The same is true with regard to sugar. Studies that have used placebos and independent observers have failed to note behavioral differences between those who ingested sugar and those who took neutral substances.

Environmental lead may be a different matter. Recent reports suggest that lead deposited in the soil from long-term use of leaded gasolines may exist in many cities. Children may be contaminated when they play in urban dirt. Lead-based paints, especially as they age and flake, represent another source of potential lead ingestion. It is assumed that if these substances are ingested orally or inhaled, they ultimately are transported via the bloodstream to the brain, where they are deposited and cause damage. Empirical studies to date have shown generally weak associations between the levels of lead found in the blood stream and ADHD symptoms. More research is sure to occur, but based on what is now known, it cannot be assumed that lead ingestion is a primary cause of ADHD.

SIDE EFFECTS OF MEDICATION

Some prescription medication can have side effects that mimic ADHD. It is known that two antiseizure medications (i.e., taken for epilepsy), phenobarbitol and Dilantin, can produce symptoms of hyperactivity and irritability. A popular asthma medication, the-ophylline (appearing also with names such as Theo-dur, Slo-bid, etc.) apparently can also cause ADHD-like symptoms. These medicines are often used for ex-tended time periods (6 months or longer). It is unclear whether the side effects of these medicines are severe enough to produce symptoms that may be mistaken for ADHD. It is important that a diagnostician knowledge-able about both ADHD and the side effects of common-ly used pediatric medicines participate in your child's evaluation.

FAMILY/SOCIAL INFLUENCES

Parents would be less than human if they did not won-der about their own role in their child's ADHD condi-tion. Many parents have been accused by relatives and friends of causing the problem by virtue of poor parent-ing. As a society we often assume that children's behav-ior mirrors the parents' approaches to childrearing. Ac-cording to this line of thinking, a one-way street of causes and effect exists between parental actions and children's behavior: lenient, inconsistent, or hostile parenting behavior leads to problems. However, objective studies of families with ADHD children have helped to correct some erroneous thinking.

Russell Barkley has cited studies of interactions between children with ADHD and their parents. Parents of children with ADHD have been found to use excessive commands and directions and to be negative. By contrast, parents of children without ADHD are more likely to allow their children to direct themselves without frequent commands and without obvious signs of negative parental attitude. On the surface this would seem to imply that parents of children with ADHD are doing a poor job, that their inept parenting style has led to problem behavior in their children. However, Barkley goes on to describe the same parent/child interactions after the children with ADHD are treated with Ritalin, a medication known to reduce ADHD symptoms. After treatment, the rate of commands and directions decreases, and the parents' previously negative attitude improves. Rather than parents' childrearing style causing their children's behavior, the opposite may be true. When forced to discipline inherently difficult children, parents resort to frequent commands, they become overly directive, and their attitude and patience suffers. These reactions occur as a result of the extraordinary demands of living with a child with ADHD; they do not cause ADHD.

Current research reflects the view that most children with ADHD have an inherent, biologically determined temperament that strongly predisposes them to ADHD symptoms. Some related problems, such as conduct or oppositional behavior, however, may be more directly influenced by childrearing. This is easy enough to understand. Conduct problems, such as stealing and lying, may be encouraged by parental lenience or by the influence of peers. Noncompliance may similarly develop if parents or teachers fail to exercise control. Of course, the child with ADHD is predisposed to these problems because of the deficits of impulsivity and inattention that define ADHD. Even when conduct problems occur in conjunction with ineffective parental discipline, the ADHD symptoms probably still have mainly a biologic cause.

There are a few dissenting voices to this current view. Alan Sroufe at the University of Minnesota has argued that ADHD may occasionally be caused, or at least aggravated, by inadvertent parenting practices. In some cases parents have been shown to interact with their children in ways that interfere with task completion (e.g., completing a building activity during play). These same parents may distract their children in the midst of activities, thus short-circuiting the development of their ability to stay focused and attend. In addition, a child who is already aroused or stimulated to a high level may be further overstimulated by a parent. Such actions, of course, hamper the child's budding competence at self-control.

Even though the role of parenting in causing ADHD may be limited, help for parents is often recommended as part of a comprehensive intervention plan (see Chapter 8). By working with a knowledgeable professional, parents may find it easier to live with their child (and vice versa). At the same time, strategies to improve conduct can be developed. Any inadvertent parental contribution to the child's problem can be addressed as well.

CONCLUSION

Although the exact causes of ADHD are not fully known at present, some facts are evident. ADHD is at least partially inherited and is not generally caused by brain injury or external factors like sugar ingestion. Rather it is generally assumed that ADHD is caused by factors in the central nervous system that are different from those existent in the central nervous systems of individuals without ADHD, although the exact nature of these differences is yet to be determined. The manner in which parents raise their children, however, is not generally thought to be a chief cause.

HOW IS ADHD DIAGNOSED?

Chapter 3

Diagnosing ADHD
by Observing Behavior

Put yourself in the role of a diagnostician. If you were the pediatrician, psychiatrist, or psychologist evaluating a child, how would you decide if a diagnosis of ADHD was warranted? You certainly would want to listen to parent and teacher comments about attention span, activity level, and impulsivity. You would also want to see these behaviors with your own eyes: you would insist on observation of behavior. In actuality, so do most professionals. As a parent, it is important for you to understand what diagnosticians are looking for when observing your child. You may thus better appreciate just what behaviors they deem essential when evaluating a child for ADHD. If your child has yet to be professionally assessed for ADHD, the information in this chapter may help you decide if an evaluation is required.

If your child has already been professionally diagnosed as having ADHD, or is suspected of having ADHD, then it is important for you to understand both the value and limitations of behavioral observations.

As discussed in Chapter 1, most of the characteristics of ADHD are observable in everyday behavior: inattention, impulsivity, and overactivity are neither so abstract nor so subtle that they cannot be readily observed. Behavioral observation is thus one important data source in determining whether an ADHD diagnosis fits or does not fit your youngster. Some diagnosticians rely almost exclusively on observational information. Of course, parents also rely mostly on observations to decide if their child has ADHD symptoms that may require professional evaluation. This chapter addresses two types of observational techniques: informal and structured.

INFORMAL OBSERVATION

There is no need to be fancy about observation, at least at the outset. Most professionals begin simply by watching the child in an examining room or their office. Sometimes children's behavior is noteworthy even before they enter the professional's office. Secretaries and receptionists naturally notice some of the actions that occur in the waiting room. Sometimes children are seen jumping wildly from chair to chair, running vigorously up and down corridors, and charging boldly past the reception area and into the practitioner's office. Such waiting room behavior is not necessarily the rule, but when it does occur, its presence is recorded.

Initial Reaction and Signs of Impulsivity

In fairness, many children do wait reasonably calmly for their appointments. Only after the session begins does much of the characteristic ADHD behavior become apparent. For many children with ADHD, clear evidence of the disorder's symptoms is seen from the outset of their contact with the diagnostician. It is surprising to many parents that diagnosticians who routinely evaluate children can so quickly establish initial impressions, impressions that often are confirmed as final diagnoses after all data are collected. Among the most telling aspects of behavior is that which occurs when a child first enters a novel environment, such as a professional's office. Sometimes, as parents are welcomed, the child bolts brashly into the professional's office to begin to explore. These children are apt to help themselves to the toys kept in the corner of a bookcase, may review documents resting on desks, or quickly attack the keyboard of an office computer. Such children are apt to talk to the diagnostician in an offhand manner, as though they were long-term acquaintances rather than someone who might, for all they know, do something unpleasant (perhaps even given him a shot). Occasionally, a child may even begin climbing precariously on windowsills, attempt to scale bookcases, or otherwise jeopardize his or her safety by careless play right in the diagnostician's office.

These actions are highly significant because they reveal one of the key aspects of ADHD—impulsivity. The child who thinks ahead realizes that although novel situations may be interesting, they can also be dangerous. As such, a certain amount of caution is necessary. The impulse to explore must be inhibited. To do so is adaptive. It is best to scan the environment, to size up the situation, and then to determine the advisability of proceeding. The behavior just described is, in many ways, the opposite of a cautious approach. It is characterized by such an intense desire to explore, and a correspondingly low regard for danger, that the child tends to react with a "Full speed ahead" approach. Although an undercontrolled approach may be acceptable in some situations (e.g., on a playground), in many situations it is neither appropriate nor adaptive. However, an office is only one such setting. The way in which the child behaves in other settings can be inferred based on behavior seen in the office, or, more importantly, may be determined by more structured observations in the classroom (discussed later in this chapter) or by interviews with parents and teachers (see Chapter 4).

Settling in and Signs of Inattention

How a child warms up to a stranger's office, and how long he or she takes to warm up, are two elements worthy of observation early on. Much more is revealed as time elapses. A typical assessment practice of including both parent and child in the office during history taking offers opportunities for such ongoing observation. Because history taking may require 45 minutes or more, an extended time is available during which to observe the child. Some children select a toy from among the objects kept in the diagnostician's office, such as blocks, and they stick with them for a reasonable interval. Other children play only briefly at one activity, then find another, and so on. At the conclusion of a 45-minute interview, the child may have tried many activities without adhering to any. Children of different ages, of course, are expected to be able to sustain attention for different time intervals. Older children who have been to school are expected to remain with a self-selected activity longer than younger children who have not yet attended school. The diagnostician watches for problems with inattention compared to age expectations. Such observations comprise one source of information when reaching conclusions about your child.

Activity Level and Rule Following

The child's motor activity and ability to follow rules are similarly of interest. Some children are quite restless even if they are able to maintain an activity. For example, many children with ADHD, especially school-age children, may sit and listen as their parents talk. Sitting positions may nonetheless be altered frequently, the child may rest his or her head intermittently in the parent's lap, may recline, tap repetitively at the furniture, or fidget with his or her foot. Obviously, a few of these behaviors are of no significance. However, frequent and intense behavior of this type, particularly after the child is directed to behave otherwise by parents, is of importance.

Inability both to adhere to a rule immediately after it has been stated (i.e., basic "compliance") and to keep track of a rule over time (called "tracking" by some experts) is exhibited by many children with ADHD. Examples seen during an extended observation may include obvious failure to abide by simple directions, such as, "Please keep your hands off the books in the bookcase." The child who continues to grab books from the shelf may have failed to keep track of the rule; thus, his or her behavior was uninfluenced by the directive. When the child intentionally looks at a parent and does the opposite of what has just been requested, then a compliance problem is probably being observed. Much more will be said later in this book about how to manage rule violation problems.

Dealing with Distractions

Compared with most environments, the office setting contains relatively few distractions. Nevertheless, some children cannot ignore even these distractions in an age-appropriate manner. Hallway noises, movement outside the window, a parent opening or closing a purse, the temperature control system starting or stopping— these are all examples of environmental changes that may challenge the child's ability to sustain attention. Likewise, the child who interrupts parents to report a bird flying by the window may have similar problems avoiding school distractions. In addition, the child who stops in the midst of telling the diagnostician about home behavior to ask, "Is someone talking in the next office?" may be unable to complete desired activities in other aspects of life. As mentioned previously, it is an accumulation of these observations that form a pattern of inattention of diagnostic significance. These and countless other instances of an inability to focus or sustain attention are seen in the office.

Talkativeness

Many children with ADHD are extremely talkative during history taking (recall that "often talks excessively" is one of the 14 symptoms of ADHD—see Table 1.1, Chapter 1). Clinicians may refer to this behavior as "hyperverbal." Empirical studies have shown that in social situations, children with ADHD are more likely than others to start conversations. This, no doubt, is often seen in office settings. Unfortunately, the same research shows that children with ADHD are more likely than children without ADHD to ignore conversation initiated by others. That is, children with ADHD are more likely to initiate social interaction, but are less responsive to social give and take. In the office setting, children with ADHD often interrupt, dominate conversations with little recognition of their dominance, or ramble excessively on irrelevant topics. Although often seen as mere friendliness by nonclinician adults, this type of behavior may actually underlie the social problems experienced by many children with ADHD. Children who are too talkative or intrusive tend to alienate peers. Through careful observation, professionals can learn much about the child's ability to focus and maintain attention, control activity, and inhibit impulses, and may draw tentative conclusions about social behavior as well.

Parents also can observe their child's behavior for this same array of symptoms. In most instances, however, objective rating forms (see Chapter 5) and a detailed history of symptoms recounted to a professional (see Chapter 4) are better ways for parents to provide input than are informal, self-interpreted observations.

STRUCTURED OBSERVATION TECHNIQUES

Unfortunately, not all professionals are equally informed and experienced, and some may fail to obtain valuable information from their informal observation. Such differences in the skills of professionals are among the drawbacks of informal office observations. Other drawbacks of such observations include: First, the office setting differs from most of the real-life settings where children play, attend class, or interact with their families; that is, the setting is artificial. Second, informal observations make it very difficult to evaluate the child's current behavior precisely enough to know for certain that behavior is improving once treatment

begins. Structured observation techniques can overcome one or both of these shortcomings.

Simple Structured Office Technique

The following is a description of a simple, structured
observation procedure used at the Phoenix [Arizona]
Children's Hospital. It can be used to supplement the
less-structured, informal techniques just described.
According to this structured technique, a child accom-
panies his or her parents to an observation room and is
presented with a task that requires concentration. For
school-age children this consists of working simple addition and subtraction problems; for preschoolers, a
simple, repetitive coloring task is presented. Children
are instructed: "Work as many problems [or color as
many shapes] as you can, keep working without looking up, and do not talk to your parent(s)."

Each child is also told that he or she will be observed by a staff member in an adjacent observation
room. An observer is positioned within this room behind a one-way mirror. The child is then given a prede-
termined time interval during which to work (in our
case, 10 minutes). Meanwhile, the observer completes
an observation form recording whether the child is
paying attention and working (i.e., whether the child is
"on task"). Alternatively, the child may be noted to be
looking around, talking, or in any other way not attending (i.e., is "off task"). To enhance the chances of two
observers' ratings agreeing, clear and specific definitions of "on task" and "off task" must exist. The 10-
minute observation period is divided into segments,
each of which is 15 seconds long (thus 40 such 15-
second segments occur during the 10-minute observa-

tion). For the first 10 seconds of each 15-second segment, the child is watched closely. Only if the child remains continuously attentive is "on task" (+) credited. If the child is off task for any part of this 10-second interval, even if he or she merely glances around momentarily, an "off task" (0) is recorded for that segment. The last 5 seconds of each interval are to be used by the observer to mark the form. A new 10-second observation interval then begins, followed by 5 seconds for the rater to mark the form. This sequence continues until the entire 10 minutes has elapsed.

Since each child has a potential of 40 segments during which he or she could be credited with being either "on task" or "off task," it is easy to calculate the percentage of either type of behavior. For example, if John earns 30 plus marks out of the possible 40, his percentage of on-task behavior is calculated as 30/40 or 75% (see Figure 3.1). Similarly, if Mary is on task 39 out of 40 times, her percentage is calculated as 39/40, or 97.5%.

Due to the brevity of the task and the absence of distractions in this setting, staying on task is relatively easy for most children. Most children's on-task percentage is far higher in this setting than in others, such as school. Nonetheless, because the technique is objective (does not rely on the observer's judgment or impressions), it serves to supplement an informal, office observation. Moreover, the technique results in a numerical index (percentage of on-task behavior) that can be used to help determine if the child is progressing once treatment begins. Behavior changes can be easily monitored over time if observations are repeated, perhaps after a specific treatment, such as medication, is started.

Name: _John Doe_

Date: _3-23-93_

Observer: _mm_

Method: _____ Point, __X__ Interval

Seconds

	15	30	45	60
0	+	+	0	+
1	0	+	+	+
2	+	+	+	+
3	+	+	+	+
4	+	+	+	+
5	+	0	+	+
6	+	+	+	+
7	0	+	0	+
8	+	0	+	0
9	0	+	0	0

(left axis label: Minutes)

Number of observations off task [0]: __10__

Percentage off task [0]: __25__

Percentage on task [+]: __75__

Figure 3.1. Observation form for simple structured observation (see text for description).

Structured School Observations

Of course this same observation technique could be used in the child's classroom. Techniques similar to this are often used by school psychologists, counselors, and teachers trained in behavior management. School-based observations are generally far more comprehensive and detailed than those used in professionals' offices. Behaviors such as attending to directions, talking with classmates, completing seatwork, leaving one's seat, aggression, and so on may be observed and their rate of occurrence recorded. By tailoring observations to students' unique problems, structured observations can be extremely valuable data sources. For instance, Wally has many ADHD symptoms, but his repeated talking-out in class is the most disturbing to classmates. If school staff were to establish his rate of "inappropriate talking-out" by using objective observation techniques prior to beginning treatment, progress could be monitored. The effects of a behavior modification program (discussed in Chapter 8) or of medication (discussed in Chapter 9) could then be objectively and accurately examined. It is extremely helpful to be able to rely on knowledgeable school personnel who can adapt observations to the individual child's characteristics. Even though children with ADHD have many symptoms in common, each child is nonetheless unique. Individualization of assessment, and later of treatment, is important.

In-class observations have enormous advantages over office observations. Foremost among these is that the child is being observed in his or her real world. When observed in everyday settings, the child's typical behavior is far more likely to occur. With other "typical" classmates available, developing a frame of reference is feasible. This can be accomplished by comparing the child with ADHD with one or two other classmates. This child-to-child comparison is important because, despite objectivity, there are as yet no standards or norms regarding how much "off-task" or "talking-out" behavior might typically be expected. For example, Zeke was noted to look around the room 12 times and to shout out unsolicited answers 4 times during a 20-minute social studies assignment. Although these rates seem excessive, without a standard against which to compare them, it is impossible to be certain that Zeke's scores are truly rare or abnormal. By watching Bill and Larry, two classmates the teacher has identified as typical, Zeke's rate of distractibility and impulsive talking-out can be fairly appraised. If Bill and Larry's 20-minute observation segment each produces only one or two episodes of looking around and if neither shouted out in class, then Zeke's problems are clearly and objectively evident.

Parents may wish to ask diagnosing professionals or school staff about the availability of objective observation techniques, both to help determine their child's current status and as a way to monitor his or her progress over time.

CONCLUSION: ADVANTAGES AND LIMITATIONS OF OBSERVATION

There is no substitute for the observations of a trained professional. It is one thing for a parent to read or be told that ADHD is characterized by excessive inattention, overactivity, and impulsivity; it is quite another to know what these symptoms look like. An experienced professional diagnostician offers the capability of observing and interpreting as few others can. Chances are that if a trained professional confirms the existence of severe ADHD symptoms during office observation, the same symptoms are present elsewhere too. The more demanding nature of the child's home, neighborhood, and school environments virtually guarantees that ADHD-related problems will occur in these settings if the underlying attention and self-control deficits exist. A rule of thumb is: if ADHD is seen in the office, it probably exists in other settings as well. However, no one observation, or even series of observations, can prove that a child should not be diagnosed as ADHD. Many children control themselves well for brief, or even extended, time intervals, but cannot duplicate that behavior day in and day out. Merely because a child sits still for his or her pediatrician or during a classroom visit by the school psychologist means little. A child who attends well in one instance may have severe problems at another instance where different, and perhaps greater, demands to inhibit impulses, pay attention, and slow down exist. As discussed in the next chapter, only by tapping parents' intimate knowledge of their children's behavior as it occurs in many settings is it possible to conclusively diagnose ADHD.

Chapter 4

Diagnosing ADHD by Interviewing

Parents who suspect that their child may have ADHD are frequently a diagnostician's most valuable resource in attempting to establish a diagnosis. The child, too, has a story to tell, although his or her self-descriptions and firsthand narrative may be less valuable than one might suspect. The job of the professional diagnostician is to elicit proper information from parents, teachers, and the child so that: 1) an accurate diagnosis can be established, and 2) the child, educational settings, and family can be understood well enough to formulate a treatment plan. Here is how the process might work.

PARENTAL INTERVIEW

As a parent, your interview with the diagnostician is your chance to tell the diagnostician what concerns you about your child's behavior. Parents should be as candid as possible, revealing everything worrisome, puzzling, or troublesome. Often a pattern begins to emerge, and this is what the professional will be listening for. He or she will be attuned to the DSM-III-R criteria for ADHD (see Table 1.1, Chapter 1). The diagnostician, by virtue of his or her experience, evaluates whether the characteristics identified by the parent in descriptions of the child's day-to-day home behavior can be matched to the ADHD symptom list. This is a crucial task. Although parents know their child, often they don't know what symptoms comprise the ADHD syndrome. Even when parents are familiar with the symptoms, they may not fully comprehend them. For example, a mother may comment that her preschool son seems to have an inconsistent appetite because he frequently leaves the table at mealtime, only to return later to nibble. The same child may be described as disinterested in puzzles and coloring, and unresponsive to frequent attempts to draw him into simple games such as Candyland. Although the parent may see little in common among these behaviors and may fail to attach significance to any of them, an experienced diagnostician may see things differently. He or she may interpret these behaviors as evidence of the ADHD symptom, "has difficulty remaining seated when required to do so" (Table 1.1).

As helpful as this open-ended conversational approach with parents may be, it is seldom sufficient. Professionals often want to inquire more systematically into many crucial areas of the child's life. Table 4.1 depicts typical areas of discussion. A full and detailed interview touching on these areas is often quite helpful. Besides detecting ADHD symptoms with this approach, the diagnostician may gain a comprehensive view of your child and family.

Consider, for example, information that may arise during a discussion of the child's preschool years. Par-

Table 4.1. Topics frequently addressed during parent interview

I.	Health and developmental data
	A. Pregnancy and birth
	B. Early temperament and development
	C. Current health
	D. Hearing and vision status
II.	Family
	A. Current living arrangement
	B. Child's role in family
	C. History of ADHD, learning or mental disorders
III.	Education
	A. School history, year by year
	B. Presence of ADHD problems
	C. Review of any prior psychoeducational evaluations
	D. Review of special services (if any)
IV.	Social/interpersonal development
	A. Relations with peers
	B. Relations with family
	C. Success in sports, organizations, and so forth
V.	Home status
	A. ADHD symptoms reviewed
	B. Conduct and compliance
	C. Mood quality, control, and self-esteem
	D. Anxiety and phobias
	E. Strengths and special interests

ents may recall that the child was "constantly on the go and into everything." The diagnostician may ask if the child was a climber or was careless around dangerous objects. The ensuing discussion may not only help establish the presence of the symptom, "often engages in physically dangerous activities without considering possible consequences" (Table 1.1), but may lead to revelations about parents' longstanding concern about their child's safety, or disagreements between parents about how to discipline the child. This information will help in developing a plan to help the child and family. Likewise, questions about how the child gets along with other children may expose the symptom, "has difficulty playing quietly" (Table 1.1), and may also point out the need to include work on social skill development as part of the child's treatment plan.

Sometimes parents and experienced diagnosticians interpret the same behavior differently. Parents who raise difficult children may develop extreme levels of tolerance for their child's actions. They may lose awareness of what typical behavior really is like. Once a parent brought her 5-year-old son in for "counseling" in the hope of developing a better relationship between him and his younger sister. During the standard intake process the child damaged several items in the office, repeatedly tripped his 3-year-old sister, attacked his parents as he became bored with the intake process, and then had a tantrum when his parents refused to terminate the session prematurely. When asked how they evaluated their child's behavior at home, the parents stated that he was "pretty easy to manage." When further quizzed about whether the child's office conduct was typical of that seen at home, the parents calmly stated that "what we're seeing right now is quite typical for him." Much of a professional's value to you is his or her experience and judgment. It is important that parents recognize this aspect of assessment and proceed with an open mind when parents' and diagnosticians' interpretations differ.

By proceeding in the listening and interpreting fashion just described, the diagnostician may mentally check off the necessary symptoms to establish the ADHD diagnosis. Of course, additional questions may be necessary to help determine if, in fact, each symptom is present. Questions about the onset of symptoms may also be asked (recall from Chapter 1 that the necessary symptoms must have a 6-month duration and must have been evident before 7 years of age).

Because children with ADHD are so much more likely than other children to be affected by conduct disorders or learning disabilities, or to become discouraged or depressed, the thorough diagnostician scrutinizes parents' comments about these considerations as well as those about ADHD. Thus, if information about adhering to household rules, controlling aggression, stealing, and lying is not volunteered by the parents, then the diagnostician will probably probe these areas through direct questioning. The same is true in regard to the child's mood state and his or her self-concept. As shown in previous chapters, this information is important in predicting problems the child might encounter later, as well as in planning how best to proceed with treatment.

Of course, parents should be questioned about their child's school status. Parents' unique ability to summarize their child's school experiences over several years is particularly helpful. For instance, knowing that a child has always had trouble with pencil and paper seatwork is a perspective that no one teacher can provide. Still, direct input from current teacher(s) is also important.

A strong working relationship with your child's physician or psychologist is essential. The assessment phase may be the beginning of a long-term relationship, and you are strongly encouraged to start by being completely open as you describe your child. The need to be candid and to trust the diagnostician is especially important during one aspect of the parent interview:

questions about the family. Family stresses related to finances, marital problems, disagreements about discipline, health of parents, parent vocational problems, and the like can all affect the functioning of a household. Although such problems seldom alone cause the symptoms that may appear as ADHD, stresses of these types can contribute to children's adjustment problems. The diagnostician may be able to offer direct help for such problems, or make a referral to other professionals who may assist you.

The diagnostician is likely to ask probing questions about the child's biological relatives, too (i.e., whether such relatives have had problems with ADHD, learning disabilities, psychiatric disorders [e.g., mood or affective disorders], juvenile neurological problems such as epilepsy or tics [nervous twitches], juvenile delinquency, and alcohol or drug problems). Many parents regard such questions as frankly intrusive or irrelevant. Yet, because ADHD is at least partially inherited, these questions may help determine whether your child is at heightened risk for ADHD or another related disorder besides ADHD. The information may also help determine whether medication is appropriate and, if so, which medication (see Irwin, chap. 9, this volume).

In addition, questions about the pregnancy and delivery, rate of the child's development, and your child's health may be asked. Comprehensiveness rather than personal curiosity is the motive behind these questions.

TEACHER INTERVIEW

Research shows that many children with ADHD manifest their symptoms most dramatically in the classroom. Accordingly, an interview between your child's diagnostician and the classroom teacher can be of enormous value. Unfortunately, however, both for logistical and financial reasons, such an interview often does not occur. Just as few doctors today find it financially feasible to make house calls, few professionals can afford to visit schools. Even telephone contact can be tricky, given teachers' busy schedules and the demands of in-office, patient contact faced by most diagnosticians.

Consequently, most professionals begin the assessment process by using general questionnaires to be completed by classroom teachers. These questionnaires can elicit information that might come from a teacher interview, including:

Academic skill level in each subject
Work habits and productiveness in class
Ability to sustain attention (especially on monotonous work)
Activity level in class and playground
Degree of emotional control
Presence of conduct problems
Social skills and acceptance by classmates
Special or remedial services now provided or contemplated

Rating forms to determine more precisely the presence of ADHD symptoms and/or multidimensional rating forms are generally used as well (see Chapter 5). Some type of reporting form completed by a classroom teacher (in lieu of direct teacher contact) is usually required before a comprehensive assessment of your child can be considered complete. Sometimes a report card or notes from the classroom teacher to the parent can suffice. If a professional attempts to proceed with an ADHD diagnosis without any information from the child's classroom teacher (assuming the child is of school age and the child is not on summer vacation, etc.), then parents may want to request that this information be included.

Depending on the style of your child's diagnostician, telephone conversations may either follow the review of completed rating forms and questionnaires or they may occur only if clarification is required. Frequently, however, as already indicated, direct teacher contact may await the beginning of treatment. At that point, the physician or psychologist may contact your child's teacher(s) to explain the nature of the problem and to propose a unified approach at home and school.

A comment about teacher reports of ADHD is in order here. Most teachers are excellent observers of behavior, and they provide indispensable information about your child. Two extreme attitudes among teachers in their reporting about ADHD are worth noting, however, even though these attitudes are uncommon. One attitude is typified by the teacher who contends there are many students with ADHD and that they should be promptly identified and started on Ritalin. Teachers with such an attitude are probably rarer than many parents believe. A thorough and professional assessment can prevent the kind of incorrect mislabeling that results from exaggerated symptom reporting and leads to overuse of medication.

The second attitude is expressed by the teacher who claims to have never seen a child with ADHD. These teachers, most of whom are well intentioned, do exist. Bias against the perceived overuse of the ADHD label probably motivates many teachers in this group. They contend that too many children are being identified as having ADHD and they want to slow or perhaps even stem the tide of ADHD labeling. Other teachers under-report symptoms in response to pressures exerted by school administrators to minimize identification of children with problems. (Such administrators fear that local school districts will be held responsible for supplemental and expensive services for children identified as having ADHD [see Chapter 10].) Other teachers believe that an ADHD diagnosis is a sentence to a life of Ritalin, and that Ritalin is an unqualified evil. Such teachers are thus loath to acknowledge symptoms of restlessness or inattention during a telephone interview with a diagnostician.

The experienced diagnostician recognizes that these extremes in attitude do occasionally occur and can factor them into the equation when deciding on an ADHD diagnosis. More important in the long run, however, is securing teacher cooperation, in case a classroom modification is later required. Providing knowledge about ADHD and offering support and encouragement, rather than confrontation, is the best way to begin the diagnostic process with a classroom teacher. Parents are strongly encouraged to avoid confrontations with teachers who initially may appear either ignorant about ADHD or inclined to obstruct an accurate assessment.

CHILD INTERVIEW

As stated at the beginning of this chapter, interviewing a child is a relatively poor method for determining if he or she is affected with ADHD. Even so, there are structured ADHD interviews for children (see Figure 4.1). Research on these interviews continues, but the interview technique has yet to be proven very effective in discriminating children with ADHD from those without ADHD. The techniques may be more helpful in adolescents and adults with ADHD.

Does this mean that child interviewing has no role in the diagnostic process? The answer is no. The interview is helpful with the broad task of assessment, even

1. Some kids find it hard to sit through something when they are supposed to. Is that hard for you?

    0   1   2

2. Do you often find that you fidget with your hands?

    0   1   2

3. Sometimes kids are supposed to play quietly. Do you find that difficult?

    0   1   2

4. Do grown-ups tell you you talk too much?

    0   1   2

5. Sometimes kids don't finish a game or something, but start something else instead. Do you do that a lot?

    0   1   2

6. Do you sometimes do dangerous things?

    0   1   2

Figure 4.1. Structured ADHD interview: child version. This form is completed by the interviewer.   0 - No or Never;   1 - Maybe some times, a little; 2 - Yes, a lot.   (Source: Selected items from *Structured ADHD Interview: Child Version,* by Barry D. Garfinkel, M.D.; reprinted by permission.)

if not effective in detecting ADHD. Parents seldom appreciate that the diagnostician must not only determine whether a child might have ADHD but also whether he or she might have a variety of other disorders that might accompany ADHD or even be mistaken for it. Especially when other information is equivocal, a detailed interview with the child can be enlightening.

Rather than discussing the specifics of the interview, some examples of the sorts of information that might emerge from this process are in order. Children who are anxious may be mistakenly labeled as having ADHD. So might a child with mood instability characterized by such symptoms as irritability, poor self-esteem, and lack of motivation to perform in school.

Although some of the external manifestations of these disorders may mimic ADHD, unique and important internal feelings and subjective emotional states are associated with these disorders. The interview with the child is designed to assess these internal emotional elements.

Contrast, for example, the hypothetical responses of a child with ADHD with those of a child with overanxious disorder during the clinical interview. When asked to describe classmates, a child with ADHD might say, "They're all right, we have a lot of fun on the playground, but sometimes they get mad at me in class." To the same question, the child with overanxious disorder might respond, "I don't really like them too much. Most of the kids call me names, and the teachers don't do anything about it." When asked to enumerate his three fondest wishes, the ADHD child might answer, "a million dollars, a party with my friends, and a Lamborghini," whereas the anxious child may respond: "to mess up less in school, to have lots of friends, to have the police catch all burglars." Information about the child's internal feelings and perceptions may thus offer helpful hints for the diagnostician. The anxious child may be restless and frequently off task, but the child's underlying problems differ from those of his or her less anxious, but equally inattentive and restless, counterpart with ADHD. Of course, some children have both ADHD and anxiety symptoms, and there are special considerations for treating these children. Efforts to differentiate children with ADHD from those with mood disorders are likewise aided by interviewing the child. Here, as with anxiety disorders, objective personality questionnaires (discussed in Chapter 5) are often invaluable.

A few children with ADHD, as well as some teenagers and many adults, are insightful and verbal enough to describe their own problems. Questions related to their abilities to control their activity level, to work without being distracted, and to avoid the impact of impulsive behavior may be telling. Of course, recognizing the subjective aspects of each individual's disorder—whether child, teenager, or adult—often helps in planning ways to circumvent these difficulties once treatment begins. Understanding of the discouragement and frustration experienced by the individual living with ADHD is best conveyed through open conversation. For many individuals, a chance to tell their own story is an important element in devising a plan to help.

CONCLUSION

The popular clinical technique of interviewing parents is indispensable in conducting a thorough evaluation of a child or teenager. Even though a direct interview with a child seldom influences the final decision regarding the presence of ADHD, such an interview can help determine the presence of co-existing problems. Moreover, only through direct discussion is the child's unique viewpoint apparent so that it can be considered in intervention planning.

Chapter 5

Diagnosing ADHD by Using Parent and Teacher Ratings

In an effort to objectify and quantify their subject of study, ADHD researchers and clinicians have developed a variety of parent and teacher-completed rating forms and personality questionnaires. These rating forms are straightforward, generally consisting of a brief list of symptoms, each of which is rated for severity by parents or teachers. The forms contain items primarily or exclusively related to ADHD symptoms.

In addition, multidimensional personality questionnaires and rating forms have been developed. These longer and more complex scales are typically designed to measure a variety of symptoms, including the ADHD dimension as well as others such as anxiety and depression. Research into the presence, severity, and changes in ADHD symptoms during treatment spurred the development of some of the popular rating techniques discussed in this chapter. The more sophisticated of these scales were constructed using elements of the logic outlined here. These techniques have gained wide acceptance because of their objective, numerical aspects and are now an important part of ADHD evaluations. Parents should expect to encounter them during the assessment process. If techniques such as those discussed here are not included in your child's evaluations, you may want to ask the diagnostician why they are absent.

LOGIC OF RATING FORMS

Objectivity

Rating forms frequently contain questions that are similar to those a parent is asked (e.g., "Is your child overexcitable and does he or she fly off the handle easily?"). during an interview. A diagnostician conducting an interview may vary the questions slightly. For instance, one parent may be asked, "Is your child easily excitable and prone to overreacting?" whereas another could be asked, "Does your child become so excited that he or she reacts too strongly and quickly at times?"

These relatively minor differences probably matter little if the goal of the interview is to obtain a general impression of the child. However, if the intent is to fix precisely the presence and severity of ADHD symptoms, this inconsistency may be a problem. Each of the three variations of the question above may be interpreted differently by the same parent! Thus, the same parent may, hypothetically, respond "yes" to the first question, "no" to the second, and be undecided about the third, merely because of the fashion in which the question is posed.

Rating forms are objective and thus avoid this problem. Hence, on a rating form, everyone is asked the exact same questions. The questions (called "items" in objective assessment techniques) are also presented in written form so that they can be read and carefully considered.

Item Selection Process

Instead of containing just one item, of course, ratings contain many. This fact allows for fuller investigation of disorders such as ADHD. Scale developers are confronted with a formidable task: to decide which items should be included in a rating scale.

One method is to ask experts, perhaps experienced clinicians, to recommend items for inclusion in a scale. This pool of items may then be sent to a committee or panel that decides which items are to be retained in the final rating scale. Some scales thus represent nothing more scientific than a consensus of opinion by expert diagnosticians.

A second method is more favorable to scientists. Rather than relying on items that merely *appear* to measure ADHD (or any other disorder), researchers empirically investigate each item's effectiveness. Promising items such as "At times does your child become so excited that he reacts too strongly and quickly?" could be tested. Two groups of parents would assist in this item tryout: one group of parents whose children have been diagnosed as having ADHD and a second group whose children do not have ADHD. For an item to have value, parents of ADHD children should, in general, respond with a yes more frequently than parents whose children do not have ADHD. Items that help discriminate children with ADHD from those without ADHD are thus retained as part of the scale, and those that do not are rejected. This method of objective, scientific item development (together with expert input about item type) has led to the creation of rating tools of great clinical merit.

Quantifying Data

Scientists are not content with imprecision. They would not, for instance, be satisfied with the statement, "Mrs. Smith agreed with *a lot* of the ADHD items," when a more numerical statement such as, "Mrs. Smith agreed with 17 of the 22 ADHD items when describing her daughter" is possible.

As helpful as it is, simple tallying of endorsed items is by itself insufficient. An even more important task is to determine which numerical values represent typical (or average) and atypical (or abnormal) ratings. It is simple to calculate the average on a rating scale. If a 22-item, true/false ADHD questionnaire were developed, all that is necessary is to study the ratings of a representative group (i.e., from the general population) of parents (and their children) and average their scores (of course, finding enough "representative" parents is far from easy). Perhaps an average of 5.1 items is agreed to by this representative group. Such a value reflects the number of ADHD symptoms present among children in general. That's fine, but how is an abnormally high amount of ADHD symptomatology identified?

Often researchers take the extreme 2% or 3% of a representative group and assume that they are unusual or abnormal. For instance, only 2 of 100 parents would agree with as many as 13 of the items, whereas the average parent would agree that only approximately 5 of the ADHD items describe their child. This rare score (the 98th percentile) could then be considered to be a cutoff. Any child whose parents agreed with 13 of the items would receive a rating above this cutoff; that is, he or she would be placed in the highly symptomatic range. Diagnosticians would use this finding, together with observation and interview information, to establish a diagnosis.

Not surprisingly, different rating forms use slightly different methods. Some forms employ ratings on a continuum (rather than true/false), so that parents rate symptoms on a range, say, from "totally absent" to "present to a severe degree." This method is equally easy to handle mathematically, because number values can be attached to each rating so that average and cutoff scores can be calculated (see examples later in the chapter). In addition, different standards must be calculated for different ages (the presence and severity of symptoms change with age) and for each of the sexes (boys are generally rated as more symptomatic than girls). It is also true that other methods of establishing cutoff scores exist, and that scales may include many characteristics besides ADHD; however, the essential logic of rating scales remains as outlined previously. I now turn to a discussion of the advantages and limitations of several popular rating scales.

RATING FORMS FOR ADHD

It is impossible in a brief volume such as this to discuss all of the available rating forms and questionnaires. The scales reviewed here are included primarily for illustrative purposes. They are not necessarily superior to those that do not appear, although they may be used somewhat more often. Frequently used examples of two major types of technique are discussed. The first type is concerned mostly with ADHD (although other factors such as conduct may also be assessed). Such scales tend to be brief so that parents and teachers can repeat ratings as treatment occurs. The second type, the multidimensional scale, is longer and attempts a more in-depth evaluation of personality and behavior. Although such scales include the ADHD dimension, they are not primarily concerned with it. Five ADHD scales and two multidimensional scales are briefly reviewed here.

Conners' Parent/Teacher Rating Scale

One of the simplest and most frequently used examples of ADHD ratings is the Conners' Rating Scale (technically called the Abbreviated Teacher Rating Scale, but also referred to as the Conners' Hyperactivity Index or simply the Conners'; see Figure 5.1). The 10 items in this brief form are drawn from longer scales for parents and teachers and are believed to be most indicative of ADHD. The Conners' is often used to assess quickly ADHD characteristics and to study changes in symptoms as treatment is applied, such as when medicine is used.

Clinicians can easily convert ratings to scores. These scores have different cutoff values depending on the age and sex of the child and whether a parent or teacher marked the form. The differing demands of homelife and school environment probably account for most of these rating inconsistencies, although parent and teacher attitudes and knowledge about ADHD can also be influential. Diagnosticians will consider these factors when reviewing ratings from the Conners' or similar scales.

Lack of parent/teacher concurrence is not unique to Conners' Rating Scales; however, the scales do have their own set of problems. For example, several of the

ABBREVIATED PARENT QUESTIONNAIRE

OFFICE USE
Patient No.
Study No.

PATIENT NAME _____

PARENT'S OBSERVATIONS

Information obtained _____ by _____
Month   Day   Year

Observation	Degree of Activity			
	Not at all	Just a little	Pretty much	Very much
1. Restless or overactive				
2. Excitable, impulsive				
3. Disturbs other children				
4. Fails to finish things he starts - short attention span				
5. Constantly fidgeting				
6. Inattentive, easily distracted				
7. Demands must be met immediately - easily frustrated				
8. Cries often and easily				
9. Mood changes quickly and drastically				
10. Temper outbursts, explosive and unpredictable behavior				

Comments : _____

_____

Figure 5.1. Sample items from The Conners' Teacher Rating Scale (short version). (Scale items are used with the permission of Multi-Health Systems, 908 Niagara Falls Blvd., North Tonawanda, NY 14120-2060 [1-800-456-3003].)

items measure conduct disorder and oppositional defiant disorder (see Chapter 1) in addition to ADHD. If the Conners' rating were used as the sole basis for ADHD diagnosis, then children with defiance and mood control problems as well as purer ADHD symptoms would be identified. Such exclusive use of the Conners' would produce a corresponding bias against children whose symptoms are predominantly inattention and disorganization but who show no conduct problems. In addition, the short form is probably too brief to be reliable (consistent).

ADD-H Comprehensive
Teacher Rating Scale (ACTeRS)

ACTeRS, featured in Figure 5.2, is a well-developed rating scale that you may encounter as part of your child's evaluation. Separate scores are available for both attention and hyperactivity symptoms (plus two other factors unrelated to ADHD). The authors' have, however, emphasized inattention over hyperactivity. This emphasis may make the scale less effective in identifying children with severe hyperactivity and impulsivity. There is also no rating form for parents. Professionals must take into account both of these limitations when selecting a scale.

ADHD Rating Scale

A rating form designed around the DSM-III-R symptoms of ADHD has been developed at the University of Massachusetts by George J. DuPaul. Called the ADHD Rating Scale, it, in essence, lists the 14 symptoms of ADHD from the DSM-III-R (see Chapter 1) and then asks parents or teachers to rate each on a continuum from "not at all" to "very much" present. Ratings can then be reviewed to determine whether the necessary 8 symptoms are present to meet the DSM-III-R criteria for ADHD. To do this, it is suggested that a rating of "pretty much" or "very much" must be checked for at least 8 of the 14 symptoms. If 8 symptoms are checked in this fashion, the child meets the key DSM-III-R criterion for ADHD. Other DSM-III-R criteria of duration (at least 6 months), onset (before age 7), and ruling out of other disorders must precede the final diagnosis.

Of significance, the scale can also be more precisely quantified. Overall ratings can be calculated for the child and compared with average and cutoff scores for children of that age, sex, and rating source (i.e., parent or teacher). In addition, scores can be calculated separately on symptoms of "inattention-hyperactivity" (e.g., "is easily distracted" and "often doesn't listen") versus "impulsivity-hyperactivity" ("often blurts out answers to questions" or "often interrupts or intrudes on others"). This distinction may help the diagnostician in identifying both children with hyperactivity and impulsiveness from the rarer distractible, disorganized child. This latter group of children may be more compatible with attention deficit disorder without hyperactivity, discussed in Chapter 1.

Like the other scales, the ADHD Rating Scale can help show change over time. It can also pinpoint where a child stands compared to peers. In fact, research suggests that so many boys manifest ADHD symptoms that a cutoff of only 8 symptoms may be too liberal for proper identification. Instead, it has been suggested that as many as 10 symptoms should be used as a cutoff to identify the truly hyperactive, impulsive, and inattentive boy. This change, suggested by Russell Barkley, has

2nd Edition

Rina K. Ullmann, M.Ed.
Esther K. Sleator, M.D.
Robert L. Sprague, Ph.D.

Below are descriptions of behavior. Please read each item and compare the child's behavior with that of his or her classmates. Circle the number that most closely corresponds with your evaluation. Transfer the total raw score for each of the four sections to the profile sheet to determine normative percentile scores.

ATTENTION	Almost Never				Almost Always
1. Works well independently	1	②	3	4	5
2. Persists with task for reasonable amount of time	①	2	3	4	5
3. Completes assigned task satisfactorily with little additional assistance	1	②	3	4	5
4. Follows simple directions accurately	1	2	③	4	5
5. Follows a sequence of instructions	1	②	3	4	5
6. Functions well in the classroom	1	②	3	4	5

ADD ITEMS 1-6 AND PLACE TOTAL HERE **12**

HYPERACTIVITY	Almost Never				Almost Always
7. Extremely overactive (out of seat, "on the go")	1	2	3	④	5
8. Overreacts	1	②	3	4	5
9. Fidgety (hands always busy)	1	2	③	4	5
10. Impulsive (acts or talks without thinking)	1	②	3	4	5
11. Restless (squirms in seat)	1	2	3	④	5

ADD ITEMS 7-11 AND PLACE TOTAL HERE **15**

Figure 5.2. ADD-H Comprehensive Teacher Rating Scale (ACTeRS), an ADHD rating form. (ACTeRS Rating Form is copyright © 1986, 1988, 1991 by MetriTech, Inc., 111 North Market Street, Champaign, IL [217] 398-4868. Reproduced by permission of the copyright holder.)

Child's Name: **Chris Student**

Rater: **Mrs. Anderson**

ID #: **71245**

Date: **3/9/93**

SOCIAL SKILLS

	Almost Never				Almost Always
12. Behaves positively with peers/classmates	1	2	③	4	5
13. Verbal communication clear and "connected"	1	2	3	④	5
14. Nonverbal communication accurate	1	2	3	④	5
15. Follows group norms and social rules	1	②	3	4	5
16. Cites general rule when criticizing ("We aren't supposed to do that")	1	2	3	④	5
17. Skillful at making new friends	1	②	3	4	5
18. Approaches situations confidently	1	2	3	4	⑤

ADD ITEMS 12-18 AND PLACE TOTAL HERE **24**

OPPOSITIONAL

	Almost Never				Almost Always
19. Tries to get others into trouble	1	②	3	4	5
20. Starts fights over nothing	①	2	3	4	5
21. Makes malicious fun of people	1	②	3	4	5
22. Defies authority	1	②	3	4	5
23. Picks on others	1	②	3	4	5
24. Mean and cruel to other children	1	②	3	4	5

ADD ITEMS 19-24 AND PLACE TOTAL HERE **11**

not yet been incorporated into the formal diagnostic criteria for ADHD, however.

Home and School Situations Questionnaires

Developed by Russell Barkley (the University of Massachusetts Medical Center), the Home and School Situations Questionnaires (see Figures 5.3 and 5.4) differ from the other scales discussed thus far. These questionnaires address where, rather than what type of, problems (symptoms) exist.

For identification purposes the diagnostician can count the number of situations in which problems occur, (i.e., any situation checked yes rather than no) or can examine the severity of ratings for various situations (i.e., whether low- or high-number values were marked). Raters may also investigate average severity ratings across situations to determine how a child compares with others at home or in school.

The Home and School Situations Questionnaires have value beyond merely assisting in ADHD diagnosis. For instance, by examining the locations in which problems arise, professionals can determine where treatment needs to be focused. The child rated most severely in social situations may require a social skills training emphasis, whereas the child whose primary problem is school seatwork may require modification of school assignments and an incentive plan to remain on task and productive. It may come as no surprise that among the most difficult situations for children with ADHD are when parents are on the telephone, during visits by company, and when the child is

HOME SITUATIONS QUESTIONNAIRE

Child's Name _____ Date _____
Name of Person Completing This Form _____

Instructions: Does your child present any problems with compliance to instructions, commands, or rules for you in any of these situations? If so, please circle the word Yes and then circle a number beside that situation that describes how severe the problem is for you. If your child is not a problem in a situation, circle No and go on to the next situation on the form.

Situations	Yes/No (Circle one)		If yes, how severe? Mild (Circle one) Severe
Playing alone	Yes	No	1 2 3 4 5 6 7 8 9
Playing with other children	Yes	No	1 2 3 4 5 6 7 8 9
Mealtimes	Yes	No	1 2 3 4 5 6 7 8 9
Getting dressed/undressed	Yes	No	1 2 3 4 5 6 7 8 9
Washing and bathing	Yes	No	1 2 3 4 5 6 7 8 9
When you are on the telephone	Yes	No	1 2 3 4 5 6 7 8 9
Watching television	Yes	No	1 2 3 4 5 6 7 8 9
When visitors are in your home	Yes	No	1 2 3 4 5 6 7 8 9
When you are visiting someone's home	Yes	No	1 2 3 4 5 6 7 8 9
In public places (restaurants, stores, church, etc.)	Yes	No	1 2 3 4 5 6 7 8 9
When father is home	Yes	No	1 2 3 4 5 6 7 8 9
When asked to do chores	Yes	No	1 2 3 4 5 6 7 8 9
When asked to do homework	Yes	No	1 2 3 4 5 6 7 8 9
At bedtime	Yes	No	1 2 3 4 5 6 7 8 9
While in the car	Yes	No	1 2 3 4 5 6 7 8 9
When with a babysitter	Yes	No	1 2 3 4 5 6 7 8 9

-- For Office Use Only --

Total number of problem settings _____ Mean severity score _____

Figure 5.3. Home Situations Questionnaire, an ADHD rating form. (From-Barkley, R.A. [1987]. *Defiant children: A clinician's manual for parent training.* New York: Guilford Press. Copyright © 1987 by The Guilford Press. A Division of Guilford Publications, Inc.; reprinted by permission.)

expected to do chores. Also noteworthy, children with ADHD have been found to exhibit fewer problems while their father is home than during most other times.

SCHOOL SITUATIONS QUESTIONNAIRE

Child's Name _____ Date _____
Name of Person Completing This Form _____

Does this child present any behavior problems for you in any of these situations? If so, indicate how severe they are.

Situations	Yes/No (Circle one)		If yes, how severe? Mild (Circle one) Severe
While arriving at school	Yes	No	1 2 3 4 5 6 7 8 9
During individual deskwork	Yes	No	1 2 3 4 5 6 7 8 9
During small-group activities	Yes	No	1 2 3 4 5 6 7 8 9
During free-play time in class	Yes	No	1 2 3 4 5 6 7 8 9
During lectures to the class	Yes	No	1 2 3 4 5 6 7 8 9
At recess	Yes	No	1 2 3 4 5 6 7 8 9
At lunch	Yes	No	1 2 3 4 5 6 7 8 9
In the hallways	Yes	No	1 2 3 4 5 6 7 8 9
In the bathroom	Yes	No	1 2 3 4 5 6 7 8 9
On field trips	Yes	No	1 2 3 4 5 6 7 8 9
During special assemblies	Yes	No	1 2 3 4 5 6 7 8 9
On the bus	Yes	No	1 2 3 4 5 6 7 8 9

-------------------------------------- For Office Use Only --------------------------------------

Total number of problem settings _____ Mean severity score _____

Figure 5.4. School Situations Questionnaire, an ADHD rating form. (From Barkley, R.A. [1987]. *Defiant children: A clinician's manual for parent training.* New York: Guilford Press. Copyright © 1987 by The Guilford Press. A Division of Guilford Publications, Inc.; reprinted by permission.)

Advantages and Limitations of Rating Forms for ADHD

Rating forms are easily used, objective, and quantifiable ways to evaluate ADHD symptoms at home and school. Because they allow ratings of symptom number and severity to be compared precisely to ratings of similar-age children, the forms represent one important element in diagnosis.

The utility of the forms is limited, however. If parents or teachers do not understand the symptoms described in the forms, they cannot produce accurate ratings. A parallel problem occurs if the rater is unfamiliar with the "normal" range of behavior for children. Thus, unless the rater has some idea how to define a "very much" rating of "excitable, impulsive" (as required on the Conners' Scales, for example), then erroneous ratings may result.

Parents' and teachers' attitude can also affect ratings and render rating tools valueless at times. The purpose of most of these scales is so transparent that markings can be tailored to the purposes of the rater, sometimes perversely so. For example, a classroom teacher intent on securing medication for a student has little trouble figuring out how to mark rating scales. An instrument like the Conners' Scale simply requires ratings of "very much" on each symptom. Conversely, those who would like to stamp out all notions of ADHD can easily mark "not at all" for each item, regardless of their true perceptions of the student's behavior. For these reasons, the rating scales mentioned here must be regarded as only one source of data. They should never be used alone to rule in or rule out the presence of ADHD.

MULTIDIMENSIONAL RATING FORMS

As their title implies, multidimensional rating forms are concerned with several dimensions of behavior and personality, not just ADHD. Thus, anxiety, conduct problems, interpersonal difficulties, and depression may be assessed in addition to ADHD symptoms. These scales have many of the same advantages as the ADHD rating scales just discussed. Importantly, however, they also allow diagnosticians to note parent or teacher reports of problems in areas that may be missed by the more narrowly focused ADHD instruments. Recall that too often parents and teachers perceive the diagnostician's task as confined to determining whether ADHD is or is not present, whereas in reality the task is to determine whether one or more disorders, including ADHD, is present. Keeping this broader goal in mind, the value of these tools is self-evident. As with ADHD scales, many multidimensional measures exist; only two commonly used examples are discussed here.

Personality Inventory for Children

In its most widely used form, the Personality Inventory for Children (PIC) consists of 280 true/false items, suitable for children from 3 to 16 years of age. Each item asks parents about an aspect of behavior (see Table 5.1). Items are then grouped into the following clinical scales:

Adjustment (overall index of behavior/emotional problems)
Intellectual screening (cognitive impairment)
Development (delayed or unusual development)

Table 5.1. Items adapted from Personality Inventory for Children (multidimensional rating form)

My son/daughter is often destructive with toys. (True or False)
My son/daughter has nightmares that wake him/her up. (True or False)
My son/daughter seems anxious about leaving me. (True or False)
As an infant, my son/daughter was seldom fussy or cranky. (True or False)
My son/daughter is cruel to animals. (True or False)

Source: From Wodrich, D. L., & Kush, S. A. (1990). *Children's psychological testing: A guide for nonpsychologists* (2nd ed.) (p. 175). Baltimore: Paul H. Brookes Publishing Co. Copyright © 1990 by David L. Wodrich. Reprinted by permission.

Note: Items in table are not actual test items.

Somatic concern (vague physical complaints)
Depression (sadness, depression)
Family relations (family or marital discord)
Delinquency (poor self-control, disobedience)
Withdrawal (social withdrawal and isolation)
Anxiety (fearfulness; excessive worry)
Psychosis (peculiar or odd behavior)
Hyperactivity (excesses in activity and distractibility)
Social skills (poor social skills)

In addition, there are three scales to determine if parents are responding fully and candidly. As with the previously mentioned ADHD scales, ratings can be compared to children of the same sex and general age group. Scores on each dimension can thus be noted as being above or below the minimum cutoff levels. The hyperactivity scale, for instance, contains 29 items from which the child's score is calculated. When approximately 13 or 14 of the items are marked as problematic, a score above the cutoff results. Sometimes, of course, scales other than hyperactivity are elevated. Perhaps a child who appeared initially distractible and restless is ultimately found to have symptoms more indicative of anxiety than ADHD.

Child Behavior Checklist

Another multidimensional instrument that you may encounter is the Child Behavior Checklist, which comes in several forms for parents and teachers. Norms exist for children from ages 4 to 16 years. Rather than the true/false items of the Personality Inventory for Children, this scale asks for ratings on 118 items, from 0 for "not true," to 1 for "somewhat or sometimes true," to 2 for "very true or often true." Other parts of the scale check for participation in school and social activities, rather than confining the search to symptoms of negative behavior or problems.

Cutoff scores exist for such dimensions as hyperactivity, depression, obsessive-compulsive behavior, aggression, and several others. Like the Personality Inventory for Children, the Child Behavior Checklist benefits enormously from its ability to detect a variety of problems, ADHD being but one possibility. The availability of both parent and teacher ratings also makes the Child Behavior Checklist helpful. Moreover, the reliability of both the Child Behavior Checklist and Personality Inventory to detect emotional, behavioral, and learning problems has been validated in many of research studies.

Advantages and Limitations of Multidimensional Rating Forms

The critical questions: "Do ADHD symptoms exist?" "What is their severity?" and "Are other problems also present?" can be most effectively answered when a multidimensional rating scale, such as the Personality Inventory for Children or Child Behavior Checklist, is used. Unfortunately, the length of the instruments prevents them from being readministered periodically to determine the success of treatment. In addition, the scales are generally limited to a search for problems. They fail to measure personality strengths, such as gregariousness or creativity, that may be helpful in planning for the child. Such information must come from interviews and reviews of the record, which should be part of a comprehensive assessment of the child.

CONCLUSION

ADHD rating scales are extremely advantageous, so much so that their use has become widespread. Especially when coupled with multidimensional rating scales, they enable the diagnostician to better understand the severity and breadth of problem behavior(s). A more effective intervention plan can thus be developed.

Chapter 6

Diagnosing ADHD from Physical, Biomedical, Laboratory, and Mental Measures

Observation, interviews, and rating forms are elements well accepted by parents in evaluating whether or not a child has ADHD. But, in truth, many parents seem to expect something much more definitive, such as a conclusive medical test. The unfortunate truth is that there is no definitive medical test for ADHD at this time. Some procedures, such as a physical examination, are nonetheless integral to a complete evaluation and may rule out other conditions or aid treatment planning. A review of these "other" assessment procedures is worthwhile and is provided here.

PHYSICAL EXAMINATION

It is generally wise to have a physical examination conducted concurrent with or as part of the interview, observation, and rating process as discussed in earlier chapters. When the diagnostician is a pediatrician, neurologist, or psychiatrist, then he or she will probably conduct such an examination. If a psychologist is performing the behavioral evaluation, the physical examination will typically be deferred to the primary care physician.

Although important, the physical examination is seldom crucial in establishing an ADHD diagnosis. For the most part, children with ADHD are indistinguishable from children without ADHD on physical examination (setting aside the obvious behavioral differences). Nowhere does the ADHD disorder manifest itself in physical differences that may be detected even with the closest scrutiny by an expert physician. As discussed in Chapter 2, ADHD is, in most cases, an inherited disorder affecting behavior. The effects, however, are not fully understood. Although empirical research has demonstrated that children with ADHD as a group have more minor physical anomalies (e.g., two hair whorls on the head and unusual skin creases on the hands), these differences are too inconsistent to be used diagnostically at present.

NEUROLOGICAL EXAMINATION

Much the same is true when physicians perform a common diagnostic procedure—the neurological examination. This examination may vary in the degree of detail and elements performed from physician to physician. Generally it consists of evaluating reflexes, coordination, visual movement and acuity, speech-language, and thought patterns to determine if brain or nervous system disease or disability exists. Most children with ADHD have entirely normal examinations of this type.

Some children with ADHD have minor or equivocal findings. These "soft signs," as they may be called by diagnosticians, are believed by some to imply subtle nervous system problems even when there is no hard evidence of damage or dysfunction. Unusual or delayed motor coordination, visual/perception problems, unusual eye movements, and poor organization of activities may be among these "soft signs." Since these signs are also present among children with problems other than ADHD, such as learning disabilities, their presence does little to help fix an ADHD diagnosis. Even more important, children who are free of learning or development problems sometimes have these signs too. Soft signs don't prove your child has ADHD.

These comments nothwithstanding, there is a valid purpose for noting soft signs. Some experts have suggested that children with soft signs should be referred for more detailed testing, such as a psychoeducational evaluation or neuropsychological evaluation (mentioned later in this chapter). The logic here is that since soft signs are associated with learning problems, their presence signals a need to look closer. In the ADHD clinic at Phoenix [Arizona] Children's Hospital, parent and teacher questionnaires and interview data permit detection of children who require more detailed psychological testing. But the soft sign method may be just as worthy. In any case, both methods allow the diagnostician to screen for potential problems. Parents should not be disappointed if the examining physician declines a detailed search for neurological soft signs. It is more important that the diagnostician have a plan for detecting children at risk for learning problems so that those who need additional psychological testing, regardless of how they are identified, are in fact referred for these services. Readers are referred to Chapter 10 for more information about learning problems among children with ADHD.

NEURODIAGNOSTIC LABORATORY TECHNIQUES

The advent of sophisticated neurodiagnostic techniques, some of which were mentioned in Chapter 2, has benefited researchers, but has had little impact on the clinical diagnosis of ADHD. This fact puzzles and frustrates many parents who reason that since ADHD problems arise in the nervous system, studying the brain with the most up-to-date techniques ought to provide important information. Unfortunately, neither the electroencephalograph (EEG), which measures electrical activity in the brain; computed tomography scan (CT scan) nor magnetic resonance imaging scan (MRI scan), both of which allow detailed study of the anatomy of the brain; nor the positron emission tomography scan (PET scan), which measures the brain's use of energy as it performs tasks, yield significant information about ADHD for the vast majority of ADHD children. Empirical studies involving these techniques have generally failed to detect ADHD with much precision, to measure its severity, or to determine its cause in the individual child. The techniques have also proved of little value in treatment planning, except in rare cases where ADHD symptoms arise because of neurological disease or definable impairment.

ROLE OF BIOMEDICAL ASSESSMENT

Physical assessment and, more rarely, the use of biomedical tests do play important roles in establishing the overall diagnosis of ADHD as well as in preparing a treatment plan, despite their limited contributions in detecting ADHD itself. The purposes of the physical examination and biomedical assessment are to: 1) rule out the possibility of a rare biomedical condition as the cause of the ADHD symptoms, 2) detect additional physical problems that may require treatment, and 3) establish whether there are contraindications to the use of certain medications (e.g., the psychostimulants discussed in Irwin, chap. 9, this volume). Table 6.1 lists some biomedical problems that rarely may cause ADHD symptoms, as well as physical problems that have been found to accompany ADHD at higher-than-expected rates. The physical exam also enables vital signs, such as blood pressure, to be measured and basic physiological values, such as height and weight, to be collected. This information may be an important baseline against which future comparisons can be made if medication is administered.

OTHER LABORATORY MEASURES

Psychology laboratories, usually located at large universities, have developed an impressive number of sci-

Table 6.1. Physical problems that may be detected during examination as part of evaluation for ADHD

Potential (although rare) causes of ADHD symptoms	Biomedical problems that occur more commonly among children with ADHD
Lead poisoning	Enuresis (bedwetting)
Seizures	Encopresis (bowel problem)
Medication side effect	Motor incoordination
Brain damage (e.g., head trauma)	Somatic complaints
Stroke	Allergies
Oxygen insufficiency (severe smoke inhalation)	Middle-ear infections

entific techniques to measure human performance. Practitioners have hoped that some of these would have clinical value in understanding or detecting ADHD and in monitoring symptom changes. However, from the long list of techniques with clinical potential, only one, the continuous performance task (CPT), has proven valuable.

The CPT consists of presenting visual, auditory, or tactile information to a subject (i.e., a child) who must attend closely and respond according to certain rules. Both subject responses (e.g., lever pressing) and the stimulus information (e.g., a series of sounds) are quite simple; the key to successful performance is to pay attention. Early research showing the CPT to be sensitive to concentration problems spurred further development of the CPT so that practitioners could use the technique in their offices.

Michael Gordon, a psychologist at the State University of New York Health Science Center at Syracuse, developed CPT hardware suitable for office use. He also devised a precise system for scoring children's performances on the CPT and conducted over 1,000 measures on a representative group of 3- to 16-year-old children to establish norms. His research has demonstrated the effectiveness of the technique in distinguishing ADHD from non-ADHD children and in reflecting changes as medication is used. Gordon's procedure requires children to sit in front of a small box containing both a screen upon which numbers are presented and a response button (see Figure 6.1). On one of the CPT tasks, each time the number 1 is followed by the number 9, the child is to press the response button. He or she is to refrain from pressing the button at all other times. Number sequences are presented continuously during a specified time interval.

Figure 6.1. Gordon Diagnostic System—Continuous Performance Task. (Photo reproduced with permission of developer: Dr. Michael Gordon, GSI, Inc., P.O. Box 746, DeWitt, NY 13214-746.)

Nine minutes has proven sufficiently long to challenge the attention of most children (see Table 6.2 for score categories and behavior measured using this technique). Because it is objective; suitable for office use; emphasizes concentration rather than the frequently measured impulsiveness, overactive, and conduct-related aspects of ADHD; complements the ADHD rating scales (see Chapter 5), many clinicians have found Gordon's modification of the CPT worthwhile. Not only is initial

Table 6.2. Elements of continuous performance task

Score category	Definition	Behavior measured
Correct responses	Number of presses when should have	Sustained attention
Omission errors	Number of missed chances to press when should have	Sustained attention
Commission errors	Number of presses when should not have pressed	Attention impulse control

From Gordon, M. (1983). *The Gordon Diagnostic System.* DeWitt, NY: Gordon Systems, Inc. Reprinted by permission.

diagnosis aided with this procedure but so too is symptom change as medication treatment is instituted.

Unfortunately, the value of other laboratory procedures has yet to be empirically documented. Techniques such as the Matching for Familiar Figures and automated Mazes may ultimately be useful clinically, but at the time of this writing have not yet proven themselves.

PSYCHOLOGICAL AND MENTAL TESTS

Like laboratory psychological techniques, standardized psychological tests, such as intelligence scales, had been regarded as potentially valuable in diagnosis. This potential seemed attainable when research on one of the most popular intelligence tests, the Wechsler scales, found that some of the subtests within the scale measured traits related to attention and concentration. Clinicians and researchers noted that children with ADHD often scored lower than other children on these particular sections of the Wechsler scales. It thus became common practice to calculate this "Freedom from Distraction" score when using the Wechsler scales and to consider the score when making an ADHD diagnosis. However, subsequent research found that substantial numbers of children without ADHD also score low on these sections, thus negating use of this Wechsler profile in ADHD diagnosis. Similar findings have been reported with other typically used psychological and mental tests: no pattern is sufficiently distinctive to children with ADHD to be of practical assistance.

Nonetheless, psychological tests are important in the comprehensive assessment of children with ADHD, even if that role is ancillary in diagnosing ADHD. Intelligence tests can help establish expectations for school learning and assist in identifying strengths and weaknesses. Specialized psychological tests of memory, visual perception, and language can likewise aid in understanding the child and in creating a plan to help him or her. Individually administered tests of academic achievement allow for accurate measurement of educational levels; children with unique learning problems, such as dyslexia, may reveal their problems during administration of these reading, writing, and mathematics tests. Cumulatively, these types of ability and academic tests are referred to as a "psychoeducational test battery." Such a battery is one essential element in determining whether a student qualifies for special education placement (see Chapter 10).

Neuropsychological tests are sometimes employed to assess children with ADHD. These tests share many elements with those used in psychoeducational evaluation (in fact, some of the same tests may be used), but they differ in important ways too. A neuropsychological evaluation is concerned with inferring brain function based on psychological test results. For example, some neuropsychological tests concern themselves with how effectively sensory or motor centers in the brain are performing. Others might be concerned with the perception of language or how effectively the brain organizes and expresses language. As valuable as these tests are in instances where there is known or suspected brain impairment (e.g., when an individual has sustained a head trauma), their value is less clear in most cases of ADHD. Moreover, these evaluation procedures are detailed and time consuming, and thus expensive. If you have concerns about the need for either a psychoeducational or neuropsychological evaluation, you are encouraged to speak to your child's diagnostician. You should speak candidly about what you wish to accomplish by such an evaluation, and be certain that there are valid reasons for including any particular element in the assessment.

CONCLUSION

Compared to diagnostic methods like observation, interviewing, and rating scale analysis, the measures discussed in this chapter are of secondary value in establishing an ADHD diagnosis. Yet, research continues and the potential for better diagnosis using laboratory or biomedical techniques does indeed exist.

Chapter 7

Case Examples in Assessing Children

This chapter includes two case examples for parents as a means of injecting reality into the ADHD assessment process. Space limitations prevent a complete reproduction here of interview information or of ratings findings. Rather, information is presented in summary form to highlight key aspects of the process. **Note**: the names of individuals are pseudonyms, and any similarity to actual individuals or circumstances is coincidental.

WAYNE

Background Information

The following information was collected during the intake process, indicating that 8-year-old Wayne was having trouble with home and school behavior. The background information described the parents' perceptions of problem behavior. Wayne's parents listed the following behaviors as present to a moderate/severe magnitude:

—Picks on others
—Has few friends
—Fights with others
—Talks back to adults
—Disobeys parents and adults
—Has chip on shoulder
—Can't sit still and concentrate

The parents' written comments were as follows:

Wayne has always been all boy. He likes rough activities and is afraid of nothing. He has always played rough, but his temper has gotten worse in the last 2 years. He has had stitches three times for falls. He drank lighter fluid when he was 4, evidently just to check out the taste. Now we're afraid he might hurt his younger brother when he gets mad. He is hard to discipline. Spankings and groundings don't work. He will lie even if caught red-handed. Wayne loves football and will watch games with his dad—about the only things he will do for very long at a time. We love him dearly and are worried about his future if this kind of behavior keeps up.

This information showed that Wayne was born following an uneventful pregnancy and delivery. He acquired developmental milestones at early ages, sitting at 5 months, ambulating independently at 10 months, using single words at 11 months, and phrases at 18 months. He was easily toilet trained, both bowel and bladder, by 24 months. His hearing and vision have been found to be normal. Wayne's parents indicated that their son was healthy and was taking no medication.

Wayne's classroom teacher listed the following behaviors as present to a moderate or severe degree:

—Does not conform to limits without external control
—Has difficulty concentrating

—Is overactive, restless, and/or continually shifts body
positions
—Disturbs other children by teasing or provoking
fights
—Argues or must have the last word in discussions
—Has tantrums
—Shows physical aggression toward objects or others
—Doesn't complete school tasks
—Is restless and fidgety

His teacher added that:

> Wayne is aggressive in class and especially on the play-
> ground. He often hits for no apparent reason. He seldom
> is sorry. He never keeps his hands to himself in line.
> The other children have grown tired of his loud and
> rough behavior. His schoolwork is completed rapidly
> and carelessly or not at all. He is often disorganized.
> Wayne has two positives. He never stays mad for long
> and he is very good in sports, especially football.

Observation of Behavior

Wayne and his family, including his 4-year-old brother,
were met in the waiting room and escorted to the corridor leading to the office. Wayne's brother edged slightly ahead of him, and it was clear that the two boys were
going to race to the office door. Suddenly Wayne hit his
brother a glancing blow to the ribs and shot completely
past the open office door and continued down a long
corridor, only to return when he saw his parents and
brother enter the office door.

Wayne's mother separated the boys as the parent
interview began. Wayne sat calmly for only a few minutes and then attempted to sit by his brother, only to be
redirected back to his original spot by his father. Wayne
looked around the room and did not appear to follow

the conversation, except periodically to add a brief comment or to disagree with his parents' statements. He seemed easily annoyed by any indication that he had done something wrong. Five minutes into the interview Wayne began to enter the conversation, in a poorly focused fashion. During the discussion of family background, Wayne spontaneously volunteered:

> Do you know what my teacher did today? She said that if Aaron got in trouble one more time he had to go to the principal's office. Aaron got his name on the board more than any other kid in our class. Aaron cannot read very well, either. He missed almost all his words in spelling, too.

The conversation was then refocused onto the background topic, and Wayne was promised a chance to tell about school later. Nonetheless, he repeatedly launched into unrelated topics and continued to do so despite redirection by his parents. Once quiet, Wayne seized large Lego-type blocks, which he repetitively popped together, separated, rotated, dropped, and flipped at his younger brother.

Wayne sat still only briefly before seeking the toys in the corner of the room—a natural tendency, although he was unconcerned with asking permission first. Several times he blocked his younger brother's access to the toys by applying shoulder blocks. However, once Wayne completed a setup of the checker game, his brother was welcomed and Wayne was affectionate, encouraging, and kind to him. The game lasted approximately 3 minutes before it was clear that it was over the head of his brother, who returned to sit by his mother. Wayne investigated several other toys and games, leaving each on the floor before resuming his original seat.

Later, Wayne and his father were taken to the observation room where he was presented several pages of simple addition and subtraction problems. During the 10-minute observation period Wayne turned and looked at his father (seated beside and slightly behind him) on three occasions, only to in each instance receive a harsh look from his father. He quickly returned to his work. Objectively, his percentage of on-task behavior was 92.5%. Subjectively, Wayne appeared only mildly restless in this situation.

Parent Interview

Wayne's parents reconfirmed some of the health and developmental information of the intake form. They described their son as a wonderful baby who adapted well to their home and its routines, developed normal rhythms, bonded well, and was a joy to them. As a toddler Wayne was "busy and curious"; he frequently attempted to climb or get into places where parents assumed no baby could go. When he learned to walk, his curiosity and activity level intensified. His parents recall that when Wayne finished playing "the room looked like a tornado hit it." They remembered their son's first contact with other toddlers vividly because he attempted to dominate others even at an early age. Competition for a toy often resulted in Wayne pushing the other child down and grabbing the desired plaything. By age 2, they noted him to be "intense." If frustrated he was quick to tantrum, even though he was generally pleasant and affectionate if not frustrated. He was likewise recalled as being easily excitable, laughing loudly during cartoons, and talking nonstop if taken by his father to a football game.

By age 3 or 4 his parents found Wayne more difficult to manage and more strong-willed. According to his mother, "If he made up his mind on something, then it was very difficult to change." Both parents were surprised that spankings were of almost no value by this time. If spanked by his mother, he refused to cry; if spanked by his father, he cried only briefly. In either case, he was apt to return undeterred to the same behavior that initially prompted the punishment. By this age, Wayne preferred to play outside. Here his behavior was generally acceptable, except that he liked to climb so much that there was constant worry he would fall and hurt himself, which he did several times. His mother recalled a frightening incident that occurred at age 5 when the family was in their front yard. A neighbor was walking two leashed Doberman pinchers down the sidewalk when Wayne abruptly raced toward them, apparently startled one of the dogs, and was knocked down as the dog snarled. Although Wayne was momentarily frightened, both parents were shocked that he showed so little apprehension about approaching these formidable-looking animals to begin with.

Wayne loved sports and was good at them. He had more trouble with indoor activities, however, where he seemed to become quickly bored. While others played board games or watched television, Wayne generally had little interest in these activities. Indoors his play was sufficiently loud and rough to alienate most potential playmates. By age 6 or 7, Wayne was reported by his parents to have few friends. Older children would allow him to play sports with them, but few age-peers ever telephoned or were willing to play if he telephoned them.

Wayne's parents were married for 2 years when he was born. It was the first marriage for each parent, and each described their relationship as good except for the strains of raising their older son. In contrast to Wayne, his 4-year-old brother was characterized by his parents as easy to discipline, although slightly overactive as well. Although neither parent had learning or ADHD-related problems, Wayne's father indicated that as a child he always preferred outdoor and physically active pursuits. He recalled his own school days as "long and boring." A paternal first cousin had a history of severe behavior problems before dropping out of school, but was never diagnosed as having ADHD.

Teacher Interview

A telephone interview was conducted with Wayne's classroom teacher. She stated that Wayne could not keep up with his third-grade classmates. Closer questioning, however, revealed that Wayne was capable of reading, spelling, computing mathematics problems, and writing adequately, but he was failing to do so. He was described as so frequently in trouble for his behavior or so careless and inattentive with his work that "his productiveness is not up to the standards of a third-grade student in our school district." Although concerned about work completion, his teacher was even more concerned about what she called "his behavior and his attitude."

The classroom discipline system, which consisted of a series of warnings and escalating consequences, was ineffective in controlling Wayne. For example, he had been warned to keeps his hands to himself, but violated that rule so many times that he had to miss recess. Although Wayne disliked missing recess, he continued to "pick at and provoke" classmates. On the playground his behavior was even worse. Here, several pushing matches had progressed into full-blown fights when Wayne lost his temper. He had been sent home from school on three occasions for these fights.

His teacher indicated that Wayne had passed many of the criterion-referenced achievement tests covering topics that had just been taught in class. In contrast, day-to-day classwork was poor. Spelling and arithmetic assignments were frequently incomplete or woefully inaccurate. Neither the school psychologist nor the school counselor had had any involvement with Wayne to date.

Rating Forms and Questionnaires

Wayne's parents completed the Personality Inventory for Children, Home Situations Questionnaire, and the ADHD Rating Scale (see Chapter 5). Figure 7.1 summarizes Wayne's Personality Inventory for Children scores. Note that both the hyperactivity (HPR) and delinquency (DLQ) scales were elevated.

Figure 7.2 summarizes all scores concerning ADHD. Wayne's parents rated him above the cutoff levels on each of the brief ADHD measures. (Note that Personality Inventory for Children hyperactivity scale scores are listed here also on the extreme right of the figure.) Among the situations where Wayne's behavior was rated as most problematic by his parents were: playing with other children; when asked to do chores; in public places; at bedtime; and when asked to do homework. These ratings were consistent with his parents' comments during interview.

Wayne's teacher assisted by completing the Teacher Rating Form from the Child Behavior Checklist, the School Situations Questionnaire, and the ADHD Rating Scale (see Chapter 5). Wayne's score exceeded the cut-

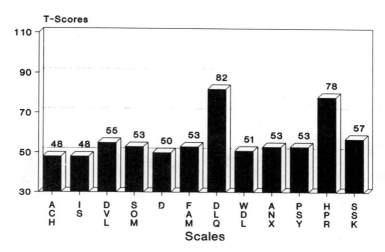

Figure 7.1. Summary of scores on Personality Inventory for Children for Wayne (case example, see text). (ACH = achievement, IS = intellectual screening, DVL = development, SOM = somatic concerns, D = depression, FAM = family relations, DLQ = delinquency, WDL = withdrawal, ANX = anxiety, PSY = psychosis, HPR = hyperactivity, SSK = social skills.)

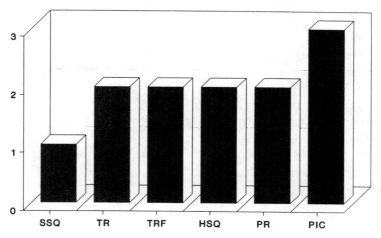

Figure 7.2. Summary of scores on ADHD rating forms for Wayne (case example, see text). (SSQ = School Situations Questionnaire, TR = teacher rating [ADHD rating scale], TRF = Teacher's rating form [attention problems scale], HSQ = Home Situations Questionnaire, PR = parent rating [ADHD rating scale], PIC = Personality Inventory For Children [hyperactivity scale], 0 = normal, 1 = mild, 2 = moderate, 3 = severe.)

off value on the attention problems inattention and aggression scales of the Teacher Rating Form, which is hardly surprising, given this teacher's prior reports. Wayne's score on the ADHD Rating Scale also exceeded the clinical cutoff.

Child Interview

After the parents' interview, Wayne was interviewed alone. At the outset, he was asked his understanding of the purpose for the visit. "I think they are mad at me for not getting my work done and fighting at school," was his response. Wayne went on to attribute most of his school problems to classmates who "start fights." He indicated that his teacher was "nice and fair." Wayne was friendly, extremely comfortable talking to an adult, and only slightly restless when provided the individual attention of the interview. Impulsivity and inattention to social cues were evident, however. Wayne frequently digressed from the topic at hand to launch into discussions about camping trips and football. He had difficulty ignoring the games and toys he had earlier placed on the floor in front of him, even though he was told that games could only be played during a subsequent office visit.

Wayne did admit to occasional difficulty controlling his temper. He also added that some schoolwork was "boring." He denied, however, problems with concentration, sitting still, or thinking before acting. As one might expect, Wayne appeared a bit more sad as he discussed loss of recesses and weekends that typically involved little peer contact. Nonetheless, he denied any feelings of sadness and discouragement.

Both the content and manner of his responses to two questions were telling. Asked what he would like to be when he grew up, Wayne responded that he would like to be a pro football player, at which time he jumped from the couch and screamed loudly, "Hut one, hut two, hut three," took an imaginary snap from the center and faked a downfield pass. He did this so quickly and spontaneously that there appeared to be little forethought or recognition that he was in an office, not a playground. When asked his three fondest wishes, Wayne responded quickly: "A million bucks, a million wishes, and no school."

Physical Examination

Wayne had recently been seen by his pediatrician. After conducting a physical examination and ordering laboratory tests, she concluded that he was healthy and that there was no biomedical problem or disease that could account for his ADHD symptoms.

Conclusions

Parent and teacher reports, coupled with the confirmatory information they provided on rating scales, allowed the ADHD diagnosis to be made confidently. The following symptoms from the DSM-III-R criteria were concluded to be present (see Table 1.1):

—"Often fidgets with hands or feet or squirms in seat"
—"Has difficulty remaining seated when required to do so"
—"Has difficulty sustaining attention in tasks or play activities"
—"Often shifts from one uncompleted activity to another"
—"Often talks excessively"
—"Often interrupts or intrudes on others"

—"Often loses things necessary for tasks or activities at school or at home"

—"Often engages in physically dangerous activities without considering possible consequences"

DSM-III-R criteria stipulate that symptoms must have at least a 6 months' duration and have been evident before age 7 years. In Wayne's case, symptoms have been present continuously since age 3 or 4 years. Wayne thus meets all necessary criteria for a DSM-III-R diagnosis of ADHD.

ADHD is only one element of Wayne's problem. Careful review of parent and teacher reports and interview data suggests that impulse and mood control elements plus resistance to authority and a tendency to blame others also exist. Despite repeated warnings, Wayne's conduct is seriously undercontrolled, especially in school. Wayne meets the diagnostic criteria for oppositional defiant disorder as well, by virtue of the following symptoms (see Table 1.4):

—"Often loses temper"

—"Often argues with adults"

—"Often actively defies or refuses adult requests or rules"

—"Is often touchy or easily annoyed by others"

—"Is often angry and resentful"

It is likely that Wayne's problems with judgment, foresight, and impulse control underlie some of his conduct problems and resistance to authority. As discussed previously, for many children with ADHD the rewards and punishments that typically are sufficient to influence behavior are ineffective. For Wayne, even repeated loss of recess, or at-home spankings, have failed to deter him. His comment that school is boring, coupled with his obvious inability to stick with monotonous classwork, suggests that he experiences deficient amounts of inherent reward for performing these tasks. Other children without ADHD problems may experience enough inherent reward in performing these tasks to keep them attending and motivated. Wayne does not.

Wayne's future is at special risk. Without changes, Wayne is likely to develop an increasingly poor attitude toward school and to further solidify his defiance and resistance to rules. Although he denies it, signs of discouragement are beginning to surface, as evidenced by his sad facial expression at times and his comments about wishing there were no more school.

Recommendations

Although the focus of this chapter is on the assessment of ADHD, it is worthwhile to conclude this case example with an outline of the types of recommendations that would be made for a child like Wayne. (Subsequent chapters offer more detailed dimensions of interventions to help children with ADHD.) Recommendations for Wayne include:

1. Provide Wayne's parents basic information about ADHD and about oppositional defiant disorder.
2. Assist Wayne's parents in developing a discipline system at home.
3. Enroll Wayne in a social skills training group.
4. Discuss Wayne's diagnosis and the need to modify school procedures with his classroom teacher, building principal, and school psychologist, as well as the necessity of providing him services under Section 504 of the Rehabilitation Act of 1973 (see Davila, chap. 10, this volume).

5. Forego a comprehensive psychological evaluation at this time, but consider one if the preceding recommendations fail to alleviate school problems.
6. Refer Wayne to an ADHD clinic for possible trial on medication.

JESSICA

Background Information

Jessica's mother was obviously ambivalent about seeing psychologists and psychiatrists about her 10-year-old daughter's "problem." Her intake information was as follows:

> I am not certain that my daughter really has a problem, but something must be done because Jessica is starting to feel bad about herself. At home she is fine most of the time, except she doesn't pay attention to what she is doing. It takes her forever to clean her room or help out with dishes. If I ask her to do something, she is apt to forget what I said and to be back asking me to repeat myself a few moments later. She must be able to read the frustration in my voice. As frustrating as home is, we could tolerate it if school were not a problem. Jessica's teachers love her, but she is almost failing. The school psychologist tested her for learning disabilities but concluded she doesn't have that problem. He felt like she might have an attention deficit or hyperactivity-type problem. Her pediatrician was unsure because Jessica didn't seem hyper in the office. He suggested we obtain a more detailed evaluation.

Jessica's pediatrician confirmed in a written evaluation that Jessica was a healthy girl and had no physical problems that were causing the behavior her mother outlined.

Jessica's parents listed the following problems:

—Spends most of the time alone (mild problem)
—Is sad much of the time (moderate problem)
—Acts younger than actual age (moderate problem)
—Daydreams a lot (moderate problem)
—Often appears to be in a daze (moderate problem)
—Doesn't finish tasks and/or has short attention span
    (mild problem)

The intake information indicated that Jessica's mother had an uncomplicated pregnancy. Labor was protracted; after nearly 18 hours a Caesarean birth was accomplished. The baby required oxygen because of a breathing problem but she ultimately did well and left the hospital when her mother was able, at age 4 days. She sat, crawled, walked, spoke her first word and first sentence, and was toilet trained on time. She was recalled to be a "busy baby who was extremely happy." Her mother indicated that Jessica had mild allergies that occasionally required treatment with over-the-counter medication. She was listed as free of hearing or vision problems.

Jessica's fourth-grade teacher checked the following problems:

—Is overly critical of self
—Does not complete tasks
—Easily distracted by ordinary classroom stimuli (i.e.,
    movements of others, noises)
—Doesn't pay attention
—Poor work skills
—Has difficulty understanding directions
—Is restless and fidgety

In addition, her teacher estimated handwriting, mathematics, and reading comprehension to be 1–2 years below grade level.

Jessica's teacher commented:

> Jessica is a sweet girl who unfortunately is falling further and further behind in class. She has difficulty keeping up with her classmates, at least partially because she is inattentive and disorganized. She doesn't listen well, yet she becomes upset (usually self-directed) when she cannot understand what to do. Sometimes she asks to stay in at recess to complete what the other students have completed during class. If I provide her easier work, she usually gets it done. Otherwise, it is always a struggle for her. The other children like her, except for the times when she can more or less drive people crazy by talking too much. Jessica seems spacey and distractible rather than hyperactive.

Observation of Behavior

Jessica appeared confident and outgoing as she and her mother entered the office. Jessica assumed the lead in answering questions, often preempting her mother's comments. Not only did Jessica answer, but she went on to provide spontaneous comments about school and homelife. Nonetheless, she showed sufficient self-control to quiet quickly when her mother signaled her to do so. Jessica scanned the room, looked out the window, and, at times, lost track of the conversation so that questions to her required repeating. The only sign of restlessness observed was repetitive sliding her foot back and forth on the carpet as her mother answered questions.

In the observation room Jessica worked mathematics problems while her mother completed rating forms.

Jessica refrained from speaking to her mother there, but she was extremely restless. She rocked in her seat and stretched her arms after every few problems. More significantly, she repeatedly drifted from her arithmetic problems to look around the room. She was off-task during 6 of the 40 10-second observation intervals (15%). Her proportion of on-task behavior was 85%.

Parent Interview

Jessica and her mother live alone. Her parents were divorced 6 years ago, and she rarely sees her father, who resides in another state. Jessica's mother said, "Perhaps as a result, Jessica and I have always been close. I know I'm reluctant to punish her because of the potential impact on our relationship. Sometimes now the closeness is too much. I feel like I have no private life." Because of Jessica's disorganization and forgetfulness, her mother has resorted to virtually constant supervision and direction. Even when Jessica was 5 or 6 she contributed little to her own dressing. At present, Jessica has to be followed around the house to assure that she brushes her teeth, combs her hair, collects her books, and picks up her lunch money before leaving for school.

Jessica's babysitters had likewise identified her as disorganized. She might pull out one set of toys, only to leave them and start with another. Her attention span was poor as a preschooler. When naptime stories were read, Jessica showed no interest. By contrast, she has always been able to flourish with undivided adult attention, often sitting and talking for extended intervals.

Jessica's mother described her as "pretty cautious physically, but pretty unafraid socially." When taken to Disneyland she avoided some of the more adventuresome rides, but started conversations with adults, teen-agers, children, or even staff, while waiting in line. Jessica's mother continued, "Even though Jessica seems so grown up when she talks with me, something goes wrong when she is with other children. She either talks too much or won't play what they want, at least for very long. Can a child be both immature and over-mature at the same time?"

Homework was identified as a particularly diffi-cult task. Despite attempts to provide structure, Jessica "invariably insists on sharpening her pencil, getting drinks, going to the bathroom, and calling me for help at the first sign of frustration. It seems as though Jessica takes twice as long as necessary to complete every-thing, especially homework." Only with detailed ques-tioning was Jessica's mother able to recall a great deal of "rocking and fidgeting when she works, even when she's getting things done." Jessica's mother asked, obvi-ously perplexed, "But still, if she were hyperactive, how could she watch television for hours on end with no problems?"

Jessica's mother stated that her daughter had re-cently shown more signs of "being down on herself." After reprimands or during weekends without play-mates, Jessica often complains of being unhappy. She has told her mother, "I know you're my best friend, but I feel like sometimes it isn't enough."

Jessica's mother concluded the interview by in-dicating that she doubted her daughter had ADHD. She stated that an afterschool tutor with whom Jessica had worked insisted that she was not "hyperactive." Jessica's mother pleaded that Jessica "isn't that much of a problem at home." She was obviously puzzled that Jessica could have an obvious problem everywhere ex-cept with her.

Teacher Interview

In a telephone interview, Jessica's teacher expanded upon the statements contained in the previously completed teacher's intake form. She expressed the greatest concern about Jessica falling behind academically: "Without better work habits, Jessica may not be ready to go on to the fifth grade." With closer questioning, her teacher was unsure about Jessica's exact level of skill development in reading, spelling, or mathematics. What was clear was that Jessica was not completing work. When questioned directly about ADHD symptoms, her teacher identified restlessness, especially in-seat movement, poor sustained attention, frequent out-of-seat behavior (pencil sharpening), talkativeness, and a lack of planning and organization. Jessica represented absolutely no behavior problem. On the contrary, she had obviously become one of her teacher's favorites. Recently, as her relationship with peers waned, Jessica had come to spend her lunch recesses in the classroom visiting with her teacher. Her teacher added, "In some ways Jessica seems more mature than her age; she can talk about adult topics almost like a friend of mine rather than a child."

Prior Psychological Testing

Because it was stored in the school's confidential file, an evaluation completed by the school psychologist a year earlier had not been seen by Jessica's mother. That evaluation found Jessica to have a verbal IQ of 113, a performance IQ (nonverbal) of 108, and a full-scale IQ (composite) of 111. The school psychologist found her to have no problems with language, memory, visual perception, or fine motor control. Equally important, Jessica's scores on individually administered tests of reading, spelling, and mathematics were average. The diagnostician noted distractibility, occasional impulsivity, and mild restlessness. A classroom observation, conducted as part of the evaluation, noted frequent attempts to talk with classmates rather than complete seatwork.

Rating Forms

Jessica's teacher and parent ADHD ratings were not in complete agreement. Her teacher identified 8 of 14 ADHD symptoms from the DSM-III-R list, with her scores on the "inattention-overactivity" dimension of the ADHD Rating Scale exceeding the cutoff level. Similarly, scores on the School Situations Questionnaire exceeded cutoff values for both the number of situations and the mean severity of those situations that were rated. Consistent with other teacher ratings were scores on the Child Behavior Checklist—Teacher Rating Form (see Figure 7.3). Here, Jessica's teacher's responses identified not only attentional problems and difficulty getting along with others but also hinted at discouragement or depression.

Jessica's mother rated her daughter as much less symptomatic on the brief ADHD-related scales. The scores on the ADHD Rating Scale and the Home Situations Questionnaire scores did not exceed cutoff values. But Jessica's score on the hyperactivity scale of the Personality Inventory for Children was elevated above the clinical cutoff. No other Personality Inventory for Children scales were so elevated, although the score on the depression scale approached significance. Her mother seemed to be noticing some signs of both inattention/hyperactivity and discouragement/depression, although less assuredly so than her teacher.

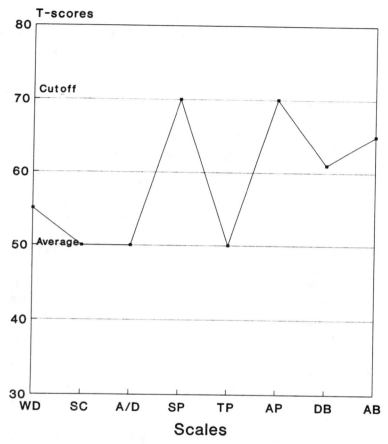

Figure 7.3. Scores on Child Behavior Checklist—Teacher Rating Form for Jessica (case example, see text). (WD = withdrawn, SC = somatic complaints, A/D = anxious/depressed, SP = social problems, TP = thought problems, AP = attention problems, DB = delinquent behavior, AB = aggressive behavior.)

Child Interview

Jessica was fun to talk with—highly verbal, expressive, and more than capable of carrying on an adultlike conversation. Yet her conversation both in style and content was too adult. Rather than telling about her school, current styles, or children's television shows, Jessica recounted R-rated movies she had seen at home, asked about the personal life of the diagnostician ("How much do you get paid at this job? Are you married?"), and wanted to know whether she was "hyper" or not. She did all of this in a fairly controlled way, with good eye contact and appropriate voice inflection. For the first 10 minutes or so of the conversation, Jessica was well focused. Thereafter, her attention wandered. At this point she interjected the previously mentioned off-topic questions and provided comments unrelated to the discussion.

Jessica was aware she was failing to complete her schoolwork. She was less sure about the presence of attentional problems, but ultimately commented, "It must be a problem because I'm obviously not getting my work done." She denied feeling hyperactive or having trouble slowing down and thinking before reacting. She stated that her clearest emotion was one of boredom, especially at school. In her words, "I really can't stand to do those worksheets they want you to do. My teacher is the greatest, so don't tell her, but the stuff is awfully boring." When directly questioned, Jessica confirmed feelings of poor self-esteem, including: unhappiness with her appearance, lack of confidence about her school ability, and concern about her capability to win friends. She also admitted to occasionally feeling "sad," only to later relabel this feeling as "boredom." She stated that she had never wished she were dead but had "wished I had never been born when I get too bored and bummed out." Jessica's fondest wishes were: to be 18, to get all A's without doing the work, and to have a new house for her and her mother.

Conclusions

Arriving at an accurate assessment was more difficult for Jessica than for Wayne. An ADHD diagnosis for Jessica was clear only after several different data sources were collected and carefully interpreted. In Jessica's case the following ADHD symptoms from DSM-III-R were noted (see Table 1.1):

— "Often fidgets with hands or feet or squirms in seat"
— "Is easily distracted by extraneous stimuli"
— "Has difficulty following through on instructions from others"
— "Has difficulty sustaining attention in tasks or play activities"
— "Often shifts from one uncompleted activity to another"
— "Often talks excessively"
— "Often does not seem to listen to what is being said to him or her"
— "Often loses things necessary for tasks or activities at school or at home"

Symptoms had adequate duration (greater than 6 months) and sufficiently early onset (before age 7 years) to allow a formal ADHD diagnosis to be made.

Several key points for parents should be kept in mind. First, even though Jessica's mother had been told (by the tutor) that her daughter did not have ADHD, Jessica nonetheless was affected by this disorder, to the degree that it was having a significant negative impact on her life, despite her mother's not being particularly distressed about her home behavior. Jessica's mother had clearly developed a high tolerance for her behavior, and because Jessica was an only child, there was no sibling in the home with whom to compare her behavior daily. Jessica's example thus demonstrates that a diagnosis of ADHD should be made only after objective and careful evaluation by professionals specifically trained to identify the disorder. Sometimes a parent's own assessment is inaccurate, as was the tutor's, who saw Jessica within a limited time frame and a narrow setting.

Second, in this example it is not surprising that scores from home and school rating forms did not completely agree. The demands to pay attention, control impulses, and follow school rules were, in Jessica's case, far more stringent at school than at home, where her mother's undivided attention, encouragement, and direction were virtually constant. Moreover, Jessica's outgoing social style, as well as her excessive pretenses of maturity, appeared to match well with her mother's desires for her daughter. Thus, Jessica was less symptomatic at home, and her mother failed to recognize some of the symptoms that were present.

Third, it is significant that only on the multidimensional questionnaire (i.e., the Personality Inventory for Children) did Jessica's mother rate her daughter as symptomatic for ADHD. The brief ADHD Rating Scales are obvious in their content and purpose. Since Jessica's mother doubted her daughter had ADHD, she simply checked her as having few problems on those scales. Jessica's mother was probably more openminded as she completed the 280 items on the Personality Inventory for Children, of which only 29 deal with ADHD. Given a more objective response set, Jessica's problems were better detected.

Fourth, a comprehensive assessment ensured that a treatment plan could also be comprehensive. Jessica was becoming discouraged about repeated failure. Thus, there were problems not just with ADHD but with self-esteem as well. Similarly, Jessica's pseudomature approach to interpersonal relations and her relationship with her mother should be addressed in treatment. Assisting Jessica to act in a more age-appropriate fashion and helping her and her mother to sort out their respective roles in the family will probably benefit Jessica's long-term adjustment.

The following recommendations would have been made for Jessica:

1. Arrange for family therapy.
2. Enroll Jessica in a social skills training group.
3. Institute a revised school program emphasizing clear expectations and limits and providing a token economy (a point system for acceptable behavior, with points traded in for rewards).
4. Refer Jessica to an ADHD clinic for a trial on medication. Because both ADHD and mood elements are present, an antidepressant or a stimulant medication would probably be considered by the attending physician. Treatment issues are discussed in later chapters.

CLOSING COMMENTS

No two children with ADHD are identical. Although they share a core group of symptoms, they differ in the manifestation of those symptoms, in symptom severity, and, most importantly, in other characteristics such as coexisting emotional, interpersonal, and school-learning problems. Each child and his or her family also possess unique strengths and talents. A thorough evaluation that includes interviews, observation, and, often, objective rating techniques, represents the best method of assessing children suspected of attentional and overactivity problems. Such an assessment permits not just the establishment of a simple diagnosis such as that of ADHD but, more importantly, it permits development of an intervention plan. Child clinicians who understand not only the syndrome of ADHD but also child development, the treatment of emotional problems, and the process of education can afford your child the optimum chance to grow and develop.

HOW IS ADHD TREATED?

Chapter 8

Behavior Management To Help the Child with ADHD

"How should I treat my child when she does something wrong?" "Was I wrong to ground my son for hitting?" "Should I back off from correcting my child so much, since I know that he has ADHD?" Questions about discipline are among the most pressing concerns of parents whose children have ADHD. This chapter addresses many of these questions. The remaining chapters in this final section focus on the other issues of great urgency for parents—how medication may help, and where and how to secure a proper education— in addition to examining interventions such as counseling and social skills training and issues in financing. For suggestions on improving your and your child's home and school situations, these chapters are crucial. I begin with the topic of parenting.

BEHAVIOR MANAGEMENT:
SEEKING PROFESSIONAL ASSISTANCE

Fortunately, a well-developed body of knowledge exists about parenting difficult children, including those with ADHD. Parents can be taught skills and techniques, called behavior modification or behavior management, that are designed to improve children's behavior. Besides offering a coherent method for approaching the toughest aspects of parenting, these techniques are empirically proven to be effective. For example, children whose parents have been taught behavioral strategies to manage noncompliance and defiance have shown significant improvement over similar children whose parents received no such training. Equally important, gains were often maintained for several years and sometimes were even extended to behaviors not directly treated, such as aggression.

One point is crucial when using behavioral techniques for children with ADHD: *techniques must be suited to the difficult nature of the child.* Research shows that children with ADHD, because they require so much disciplining, often tax parenting skills severely and sometimes force parents into heavy-handed discipline. Although many "how-to" parenting books exist, their strategies are aimed at temperamentally easy children—those with flexibility, an even temper, and a desire to please. Few such books are adapted for parents of truly difficult children. As discussed in Chapter 1, many children with ADHD are strong-willed and noncompliant, and have explosive tempers. Thus, most basic behavior management guidebooks may leave parents of children with ADHD frustrated because the straightforward behavior-change techniques they espouse backfire when applied to children with ADHD.

Parents of children with ADHD often find they need face-to-face meetings with a professional to help decide how to discipline. Indeed, rather than relying on general, and necessarily superficial, outlines of behavioral techniques, *many parents find success only when a trained behavioral therapist, such as a psychologist or counselor trained to work with ADHD children, assists them.* Sometimes a professionally led parent-training group is sufficient. At other times individual sessions are required to ensure that basic principles are understood, that implementation fits family circumstances, and that the disciplinary plan is "working."

The material following is designed to provide you, as parents, with some basic behavior modification ideas and techniques. If your child's problems are relatively mild, these techniques may be attempted after reading the material. At Phoenix [Arizona] Children's Hospital, the information following is given to parents to read before beginning work on behavior management with an individual therapist. If your child has more severe problems, it is suggested the material be read prior to working with a professional who can tailor a program to your unique circumstances. These ideas may seem simple, but implementing them can be extremely difficult without professional assistance.

BASIC IDEAS IN BEHAVIOR MANAGEMENT

Behavior management's most basic idea is that children, like all other humans and animals, learn many of their behaviors from their environment. Children with ADHD, although compromised by impulse control and attending problems, nonetheless learn many behaviors from the world around them. Just as some unacceptable behaviors are learned from the environment, they can also be unlearned and more-acceptable behaviors learned to take their place.

Why are some behaviors learned and others not? A partial answer to that question is simply that learned behavior works. Behaviors that result in consequences deemed desirable by the individual are likely to be retained or strengthened and may ultimately become habitual. Behaviors that result in undesirable consequences are likely to be discarded or weakened. What each individual experiences as a consequence of his or her actions determines, at least to some extent, whether the individual will attempt that behavior again. For the most part, all humans are pragmatic. This includes children with ADHD.

The following simple example can explain why children sometimes behave as they do. Jeremy is the class clown. Each time he makes a burping noise several classmates laugh. Jeremy's behavior (burping) is followed by desirable consequences (attention from peers, laughter), which strengthens this behavior and heightens its probability of recurring. From the teacher's viewpoint, the behavior is unacceptable, but from Jeremy's viewpoint it works because he receives a positive consequence. Despite adults' wishes to the contrary, this behavior is thus likely to continue unless changes are made in the consequences Jeremy receives for burping.

It is easy to see how a behavior change program for Jeremy may be instituted. If he is burping to make classmates laugh, he can be induced to stop burping if classmates ignore this behavior. A simple plan to encourage inattention to Jeremy at these times could be implemented. Although Jeremy may not like this new arrangement, and even though he has not changed his mind about inappropriate attention seeking, he nevertheless may cease this bad behavior. *This focus on changing behavior, rather than on changing attitudes or thought patterns, is a cornerstone of the behavior management approach.*

You should also note that this strategy altered Jeremy's behavior but not his hyperactivity or inattention. Behavior management techniques are valuable because they improve behavior. This point not withstanding, they have limited utility because they leave the underlying attention and concentration problems unremedied. *You can expect behavioral management techniques to improve your child's behavior, but do not hope that they will alleviate your child's ADHD condition. Alone, they will not. In combination with proper educational placement, carefully prescribed medication, and adjunctive services such as social skills training for children who require it, these procedures may help enormously.* This fact is especially true if your child has symptoms of conduct disorder or oppositional defiant disorder accompanying ADHD (see Chapter 1).

STEPS IN USING BEHAVIOR MANAGEMENT

If you choose to work with a mental health professional, he or she will probably address two points before sharing behavioral strategies with you. If you are not working with such a professional, you are still encouraged to consider these two points before proceeding on your own.

First, it is essential to identify which of your child's behaviors are primarily symptoms of his or her

ADHD condition. These behaviors will probably be quite difficult, if not impossible, to change by using behavioral strategies. For example, a behavioral strategy designed to teach a 6-year-old with ADHD to sit still and attend to a 1-hour church service is destined to fail and invites failure and frustration for all those involved.

Second, parents' personal or marital problems may prevent the sound use of behavioral techniques. Obviously, if spouses disagree on discipline or if they are preoccupied with other friction points in their relationship, then these techniques will be hard to use effectively. Individual or marital help may be necessary if either problem is present. In many of these instances, behavioral training is best postponed until individual or marital issues resolve. Provided that parents understand the manifestations of ADHD and are reasonably free of personal or marital problems, then learning behavioral techniques can begin.

In its simplest form, behavior management involves responding to the following four questions:

1. What is the problem behavior I would like to eliminate?
2. What behavior would be more acceptable?
3. What are the consequences of the problem and target behaviors?
4. How can I rearrange consequences to discourage problem and encourage target behaviors?

Each of these questions is discussed in the subsections following.

Identify Problem Behavior

The first question, *"What is the problem behavior I would like to eliminate?"* is easily answered by most parents. As examples: "I would like to see my son hit less." "I wish my daughter would stop ignoring my requests and refusing my directions." Both of these statements are good because they answer the question simply. A simple answer helps parents keep in mind what they are trying to reduce or eliminate. Vague answers or those that address attitudes, thoughts, or feelings are less valuable, such as: "I wish my child's attitude about life would improve." "My goal is to get my child to like himself and others more." These are laudable goals, but they are no help in developing a behavior change program. How would one know that "attitude about life" is better? Could spouses each agree on what "liking himself" really means? Probably not. In contrast, a behavior—such as hitting—is readily understood and recognized by all those involved, including the child.

Identify Target Behavior

The second question, *"What behavior would be more acceptable?"* requires more thought. The answer to this question is called the target behavior (it is what we are shooting for). Here parents often draw blanks. Although hitting or refusing parental requests are unacceptable, specifying what is acceptable may be puzzling, at least until parents become accustomed to explicitly identifying what they would like to see changed. Yet, being clear about what behavior is hoped for is crucial. Simply put, if we don't know what behavior we want to achieve, we are unlikely to achieve it. Regarding hitting, for example, "keeping hands to self" is a more acceptable alternative than hitting. In fact, the problem would be solved if the child kept his hands to himself; by doing so he would be incapable of hitting.

Identify Consequences of Each Behavior

The third question now goes to the heart of behavior change, "*What are the consequences of the problem and target behaviors?*" To answer this question parents are sometimes helped by stepping outside their point of view and assuming that of their child. Consider the example of Juan, a boy whose problem is excessive hitting. The following episode occurred between Juan and his brother.

Juan and his brother were watching television.
Juan hit his brother.
Hitting was followed by immediate screams from his
　　brother and reprimands from parents.

When Juan and his brother watch television peaceably, there is little interaction with each other or with parents. One can thus draw hunches about possible consequences and their effects. In this case, it is hypothesized that Juan sees few consequences for sitting peaceably with his brother. Figure 8.1 illustrates the consequences of hitting versus keeping hands to self. A plus (+) stands for a positively perceived consequence, and a zero (0) stands for no consequence. Note that a

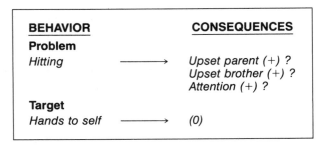

Figure 8.1. Initial consequences of problem behavior (hitting) versus target behavior (hands to self) ([+], positive consequence; [0], no consequence).

zero (0) is listed for sitting nicely with hands to self. In contrast, note the obvious consequences of hitting: upset parent, upset brother, parental attention. Note, too, that these follow immediately on the heels of misbehavior. One might guess, without knowing for certain, that those consequences are rewarding for Juan. Why particular consequences are rewarding is unimportant—the fact that the child appears to seek them is all that matters at this point. If these suppositions are true, then there is little doubt about why this behavior occurs—it works well for Juan. The next subsection suggests a way to resolve the problem.

Rearrange Consequences

"How can I rearrange consequences to discourage problem and encourage target behavior?" is the fourth question. Rearranging consequences generally involves altering the immediate consequences so that they come to favor target rather than problem behavior. There are many ways to accomplish this. Juan's example is again used here to briefly explain this process; various types of positive and negative consequences are then discussed more fully in subsequent sections. In this example, reducing positive consequences for Juan's problem behavior may be a first step. As such, parents may be encouraged to avoid rushing into conflicts or, at least, to minimize discussion once they are involved in conflicts between the brothers. Likewise, arranging for less screaming by the brother may help. Both of these measures are designed to reduce the chance of positive consequences following the problem behavior. Additional simple approaches may include adding positive consequences when target behaviors occur. "I like the way you are sitting with your hands to yourself." Or

perhaps using privileges—"Juan, since you did a good job keeping your hands to yourself, you can ride in the front when we go pick up your sister" (assuming riding in the front seat is desirable). Simple approaches like this may tip the scale so that there are more positives for target behavior than for problem behavior. Over time these arrangements ought to help discourage problem behaviors and encourage target behavior.

Unfortunately, this plan would fail miserably for many children unless negative consequences were used. Many children with ADHD respond only briefly and undramatically to praise or other positives. Likewise, negative consequences work only briefly and less dramatically for children with ADHD than they do for other children. The very bases of reward and punishment may operate slightly differently for these children. An immediate negative consequence for continuing the hitting, such as isolation in time-out (discussed in the next section) would probably be required to deter this behavior. Hence, time-out is listed as a negative (−) following hitting in Figure 8.2. Note that with this rearrangement of consequences, target behavior suddenly becomes more advantageous to the child, where-

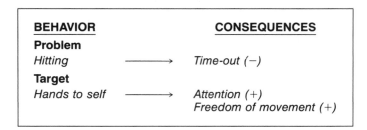

Figure 8.2. Rearrangement of consequences in Figure 8.1 so that target behavior becomes more advantageous to the child ([−], negative consequence; [+], positive consequence).

as problem behavior becomes less advantageous. Although not the entire solution to misbehavior, such rearrangement often helps to improve behavior substantially, especially when used repetitively and systematically. More will be said later about using behavioral techniques as an overall approach to discipline. We next turn to positive and negative consequences that typically work, to provide you with at least beginning ideas.

POSITIVE CONSEQUENCES

Parents often mistakenly assume that the use of positives must involve purchasing candy and using it as a bribe to get their child to do as they are told. This is not advocated here. Instead, the general notion is to use already-available privileges—things perceived as pleasurable by the child—as a way to encourage good behavior. Many of these positives are social in nature; they are not tangible. *Attention from parents, siblings, or peers is often the most powerful and easily accessed positive consequence.*

Unfortunately, there are not universally positive consequences. It all depends on how your child reacts to them. For example, most children love to be praised, but some hate it. Furthermore, even children who typically respond well to praise may prefer to forgo it under certain circumstances. They may not want to be told "good job" when peers are present, by someone with low popularity, or when praise is attempted by someone with whom they are unhappy (e.g., by parents immediately after a fight has occurred). Most children would also prefer that their parents not be too angry with them, although at times they may desire to annoy parents so ardently that they will withstand parental anger. Thus, at times, an upset parent may actually be a positive consequence, even though most of the time it would be a negative one. These warnings about over-generalization not withstanding, some general ideas for positives follow.

Attention as a Positive Consequence

Wendy talks rudely—that is the problem behavior. Her mother wants her to talk more politely—that is the target behavior. At present, the consequences for both polite and rude talk are continuing discussion with her mother (see Figure 8.3). That is, no matter how rudely Wendy talks, her mother continues to talk with her. Like most parents, however, Wendy's mother has told her that she shouldn't talk rudely and has provided her daughter a detailed rationale for why talking like this is a poor idea. Wendy's mother makes a common error: she attempts to discipline primarily with words rather than action. Her wordy discussions inadvertently provide Wendy attention as she misbehaves or immediately afterwards. A change is required.

We might suggest a simple plan whereby positive consequences are used to promote the target behavior—polite talk. Wendy's mother might be encouraged to say

BEHAVIOR	CONSEQUENCES
Problem	
Rude talk $\longrightarrow$	*Attention (+)*
Target	
Polite talk $\longrightarrow$	*Attention (+)*

Figure 8.3. Initial consequences of rude talk versus polite talk ([+], positive consequence).

something like: "I'm sorry, but I find rude talk unacceptable. If you continue to talk rudely, I will no longer talk with you. If you talk politely, I will be happy to talk with you." She may then either leave the area or direct her attention away (cease to make eye contact and cease to talk) if Wendy persists with rude talk. Since the goal is to encourage polite talk, as soon as Wendy switches to polite talk her mother would immediately return her full attention to her daughter. Obviously in this situation there is one very powerful positive consequence—mother's attention. By this arrangement, problem behavior is no longer followed by a positive consequence; only acceptable (target) behavior is followed by these consequences (see Figure 8.4).

This strategy has a good chance of working, for several reasons. First, Wendy probably knows how to do the target behavior—she merely has neglected to do so at this point or has purposely chosen to do otherwise. Second, there are immediate powerful consequences for doing the target behavior.

But there are practical problems too. First, Wendy's behavior is likely to become worse (more intense, more dramatic, or more threatening) before it improves. This is a well-known occurrence when old ways of behaving

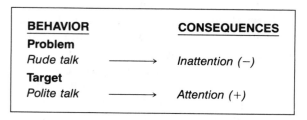

Figure 8.4. Rearrangement of consequences in Figure 8.3 so that target behavior becomes more advantageous ([−], negative consequence; [+], positive consequence).

are disrupted. If parents are unable to withstand the child's temporarily worsening behavior, then this particular strategy is not recommended. Second, some parents would find the worsened behavior almost impossible to ignore. Still other parents would disagree with using this technique, considering it rude or unkind. In these cases, alternative techniques would be sought out. Again, behavior management provides methods for understanding why behaviors occur and for finding simple ways to change the behavior. Although the behavior-change plans are not always usable, a logical approach to discipline problems often helps parents understand why behavior occurs and how it might be changed.

Preferred or Habitual
Activities as Positive Consequences

Most parents fail to recognize an array of powerful consequences capable of motivating desired behavior. These are activities the child is already doing, is anticipating doing soon, or would do soon if given a chance.

Ross and his brother Rick chronically fight in the car. Their parents described the problem as: yelling, hitting, and getting out of seatbelts. Target behaviors were identified as: inside voice, hands to self, and remaining in seatbelt. It was realized that the boys may enjoy annoying their parents, but other positive and negative consequences were not obvious. Worse, parents could not think of immediate consequences capable of improving behavior (see Figure 8.5). It was then suggested that the boys might prefer traveling to their destination rather than waiting in a stationary car. A moving vehicle is often pleasurable compared to a

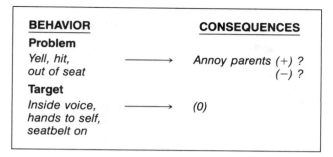

Figure 8.5. Initial consequences of fighting in car ([+], positive consequence; [−], negative consequence; [0], no consequence).

stopped one. If so, it could potentially be used to motivate behavior change.

Ross and Rick's parents instructed the boys as they entered the car, "Rules for riding are that everyone must have a fastened seatbelt, use inside voice, and keep hands to themselves. As long as you do, the car will keep moving. If you don't, we may have to stop and wait until everyone is following the rules." Now there is a significant inducement to follow rules because positive consequences follow immediately (in fact simultaneously) upon good behavior. Problem behavior receives an immediate negative consequence (see Figure 8.6). Again, parents may complain that this arrangement is unfair to the child who was not at fault, or to themselves as innocent bystanders. Or, perhaps, it will be suggested that children will not find stopping in the car unpleasant. Typically they do, however, provided parents carefully avoid attending to them while stopped. The point remains, however, that thinking of consequences in a systematic way helps generate solutions that can be tested to determine their effectiveness.

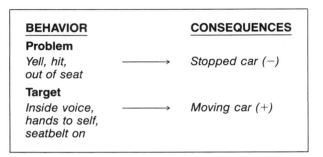

Figure 8.6. Rearrangement of consequences in Figure 8.5 so that target behavior becomes advantageous ([−], negative consequence; [+], positive consequence).

A similar, and even more common, example is evident when children transition from one activity to another. Here there is often a strong desire to get on with the next activity. For example, children about to go out to recess may push or crowd in line. Wise teachers often say, "As soon as everyone is lined up straight, is looking at me, and is quiet, we will be able to go outside." Children generally shape up quickly with such a strong immediate positive consequence awaiting their compliance.

Privileges and Rewards in a Formal Positive Consequence System

Sometimes positive consequences are helpful in developing good habits, rather than dealing with pressing discipline problems as they arise. If a clear list of wished-for target behaviors exists (learn to make bed and clean room, complete homework on time, etc.), and if strongly motivating privileges or rewards are identifiable, developing a formal system may be worthwhile. Sometimes a briefly written list of behaviors and privileges is sufficient. If the child completes all home-work each night by 7:00, then an extra hour of free time is earned. This arrangement should ideally remain in place for at least several weeks or months as a way to help develop the habit of prompt homework com-pletion.

More formal and complicated systems also work well for some children. Sometimes these are referred to as token economies. Figure 8.7 outlines an agreement between Janet, a teenager with ADHD, and her parents. Target behaviors include: clothes and books laid out for school each evening and room clean each day (i.e., bed made, floor picked up, and dirty clothes in hamper). For each behavior that is completed in an acceptable fashion, points are earned. These are tradable for privi-leges and rewards listed on the reward menu. Prepared forms are easily used to list both target behaviors, points awarded, and reward menu (see Figure 8.7). Older children work well with points. Younger chil-dren may require actual tokens that can be traded for privileges, in lieu of points.

Although these programs have been shown to im-prove behavior, they are not without some practical drawbacks. First, if considering using a system like this, you must decide what you hope to accomplish. For many families, long-term change is sought and a long-term commitment to the system may be necessary. Many families find adhering to this type of arrange-ment difficult in the long run. In addition, many par-ents fail to provide a rich enough array of privileges, or their trade-ins are too remote or too infrequent, or they place too many behaviors on the target list. Formal sys-tems, thus, are generally best used in collaboration with a counselor or psychologist familiar with your child and family, at least in the beginning.

Home Reward Program

Name: Janet Date: 12-13 to 12-19

Target Behaviors: #1 Room clean = 1 pt. each #2 Ready in evening = 1 pt. each

	#1 Room clean = 1 pt. each	#2 Ready in evening = 1 pt. each
Monday	1	1
Tuesday	0	0
Wednesday	1	0
Thursday	1	1
Friday	0	
Saturday	1	
Sunday	1	1
POINTS:	5	3

MENU:
Movie	= 5	Points
Extra allowance	= 2	Points
Late night	= 5	Points
Special snack	= 1	Points

Figure 8.7. Example of token economy reward system (zero [0], no points).

Prompt, Positive Consequences

Even our best efforts at using positive consequences may fail. Parents then naturally question whether behavior management really works. In most instances, it is the way behavioral techniques are applied, rather than the principles themselves, that is faulty. When failure occurs, two possible remedies are suggested. The first is to use more immediate consequences, and the second is to use a behavioral principle called shaping (discussed in the next subsection).

Regarding prompt consequences, we adults are accustomed to looking at the world in one way, children probably in another. For us, the end of this week seems quite immediate. If told by a supervisor that increased work hours on Monday would result in a cash bonus on Friday afternoon, we would probably think about this impending consequence, and we might well extend our workday. Many children, in contrast, would respond less dramatically. If told on Monday morning, for example, to increase school productiveness to receive positive consequences on Friday, many children would not do so. Friday seems too remote to have much impact on Monday's or Tuesday's behavior.

Prompt consequences are generally even more important for children with ADHD. Recall that a cardinal feature of ADHD is impulsivity, or an inability to plan carefully before acting. Impulsivity also means that immediate actions that the child finds fun or interesting influence behavior more than remote consequences. Thus, poking at a classmate who walks by is more inviting than holding hands back and adhering to class rules. The prospect of punishment for poking fails to offset the immediate fun of doing it. Children with ADHD seem even less able to anticipate delayed consequences. In recognition of that fact, parents do well to follow good behavior with positive consequences as quickly as possible. At times, these consequences must be truly immediate.

Dale loved to watch *Sesame Street* on television. His mother ardently desired that he place his dirty dishes in the sink and return the milk to the refrigerator after finishing breakfast. Recognizing the value of positive consequences, Dale's mother told him that if he put his dishes in the sink and the milk in the refrigerator (target behavior), then he could watch *Sesame Street* (positive consequence). Failure to do these things (problem behavior) would result in no television (negative consequence). Unfortunately, Dale consistently failed to do these two things, appearing totally unconcerned about television until a few minutes before his beloved program began, at which time he invariably would have a tantrum when told he had not earned access to *Sesame Street*. Dale wished to earn this privilege, and he certainly knew how to do the desired behavior. He simply failed to anticipate upcoming consequences, even with his mother's reminders (see Figure 8.8).

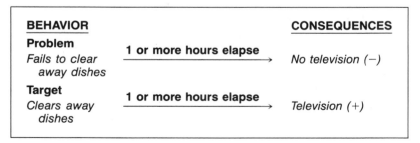

BEHAVIOR		CONSEQUENCES
Problem *Fails to clear away dishes*	1 or more hours elapse ⟶	*No television (−)*
Target *Clears away dishes*	1 or more hours elapse ⟶	*Television (+)*

Figure 8.8. Long intervals between target behavior (clearing away dishes) and positive consequence may be an insufficient motivation for young children ([−], negative consequence; [+], positive consequence).

An alternative plan emphasizing immediate consequences was used. Dale's mother recorded Monday's edition of *Sesame Street* on the VCR while she and Dale were on an outing. On Tuesday he was offered Monday's program immediately upon performing the desired behaviors: "Dale, as soon as you put dishes and milk away you can watch your program." This deal quickly induced Dale to execute his chores, whereupon he raced for the television set. Contrast the promptness of consequences for the first and second programs in Figures 8.8 and 8.9.

Shaping New Behavior through Positive Consequences

Shortening the interval between target behavior and positive consequences may not suffice, however. When children do not yet possess the desired actions in their array of available behaviors, then a behavioral plan that teaches as well as motivates may be required. Consider the example of Kim, a 4-year-old with ADHD.

Kim's parents had read about behavior modification and hoped to improve her conduct in the grocery store—an area long plagued by problems—by devising

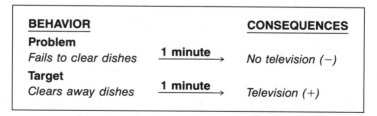

Figure 8.9. Shortening the interval in Figure 8.8 between target behavior and positive consequences brings compliance ([−], negative consequence; [+], positive consequence).

a behavioral plan. Kim's parents began correctly by explicitly identifying problem behaviors—running away from them and grabbing items. After considering all potential positive consequences, the parents devised a plan whereby rather than putting candy in the cart first, as had been their custom, they would make buying candy contingent upon Kim's exhibiting appropriate, target behavior: "Kim, if you hold on to the cart all the way through the store, then Mommy and Daddy will get candy before we leave." It didn't work, however. Kim had never learned to hold on to the cart for more than 10 or 15 seconds, yet her parents started with a plan that required her to do it for more than 30 minutes!

Shaping, or teaching new behavior by successive approximations, can help. Instead of shooting for the difficult, final target behavior, the shaping technique begins with small successes that approximate the target, and then slowly builds upon them in the hope of eventually reaching the final goal. Positive consequences are used to provide motivation and to signal to the child that he or she is on the correct path of learning.

Using this strategy, Kim's parents developed a plan aimed at extremely small amounts of target behavior, each of which was to be followed immediately by a positive consequence. After receiving directions, Kim was awarded a small piece of candy if she walked with her hand on the cart for the distance of one-half of one grocery store aisle. She was also encouraged with praise, "Good job of holding on like a big girl, Kim!" But she could earn no more candy until she had traversed another half aisle with her hand on the cart. This same procedure was employed, in half-aisle increments, throughout the grocery shopping trip. One step at a time, Kim proceeded through the entire store hold-

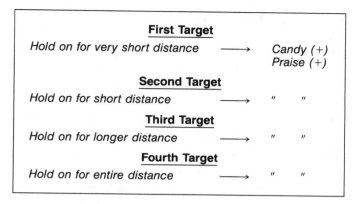

First Target

Hold on for very short distance ⟶   *Candy (+)*
                                                Praise (+)

Second Target

Hold on for short distance ⟶   "   "

Third Target

Hold on for longer distance ⟶   "   "

Fourth Target

Hold on for entire distance ⟶   "   "

Figure 8.10. Using shaping to teach new behavior (holding on to grocery cart in store) ([+], positive consequence).

ing on to the cart. This was her small initial goal and she was successful in meeting it.

The demand for success was then slowly increased. A standard of one entire aisle while holding on was established. Once this was mastered, a new standard of several aisles without interruption, to be traded for several pieces of candy, was established and ultimately mastered within a few grocery store visits. Unfortunately, Kim's age and the severity of her overactivity prevented her from walking all the way through the store prior to earning a reward. This is an extremely difficult task for this child; expectations may have to be reduced. Nonetheless, the approach of slowly building skills one step at a time by using available consequences offers much help to parents (see Figure 8.10).

NEGATIVE CONSEQUENCES

Without negative consequences to help curtail their unacceptable behavior, many children with ADHD would be unmanageable. Unfortunately, when it comes to using negative consequences, many parents have trouble. Parents are apt to select the wrong negative consequence or to implement it incorrectly or at the wrong times. Part of the problem stems from our unavoidable emotional involvement with our children. After all, as parents we are only human. A portion, however, stems from mistaken ideas about how and why negative consequences work.

Spanking as a Negative Consequence

To spank or not to spank, that is the question parents often ask. Rather than searching for a right or wrong answer, it is often more important, I believe, to investigate the rationale behind spanking. *If* there is a rationale for spanking, it ought to be that spanking is a viable negative consequence. According to that line of thinking, we are attempting to convey a point to the child: If you play too roughly, then you will be spanked. Hypothetically, the repeated use of this negative consequence offers the hope of discouraging unacceptable behavior such as rough play.

Once the rationale is understood, the practical question of implementing spanking must be examined. Parents might ask themselves how many times per day they are willing to spank their child. Few parents answer more than one or two. They next might ask themselves how many times per day might their child misbehave—that is, how many times might a negative consequence be required. Few parents would answer one to two; most indicate 15, 20, or 30. An inequity is thus evident between those behaviors that potentially merit negative consequences and the family's ability to use spanking as a consequence. If, for example, a child engages in 10 potentially punishable behaviors per day but knows parents will spank only once, then only a 10 percent chance of a negative consequence exists. Why not misbehave and live with the 90% chance that a negative consequence will not be forthcoming? Setting aside the potential disadvantages of parents' modeling unacceptable behavior and the potential damage to self-esteem inherent in doing it, spanking simply fails to work as a consistent deterrent for most children with significant behavioral problems. Most children with ADHD simply misbehave too much to allow the spanking to work.

Time-Out as a Negative Consequence

For many families, time-out proves to be a more usable consequence, and thus a more credible deterrent.

Many parents mistakenly assume that time-out is a place, such as a time-out chair. In reality time-out is a principle, the particulars of which need to be suited to each child and circumstance. The time-out principle rests on the idea that if a child is where the action is, where it is stimulating, and where he or she prefers to be, then a temporary loss of the privilege can be used as a mild punishment or negative consequence. Usually a corner, an isolated area marked by tape on the floor, or a sparsely filled spare room works best. Since the idea is to reduce stimulation and make the consequence uninteresting, parents must take care not to pay too much attention when using this consequence. Thus, lecturing on misbehavior as the child is sent to time-out or responding to the child's comments while he or she is in time-out should be avoided to the extent possible. This is often difficult, as children dislike the boredom of time-out and seek to lessen it by engaging parents, often in clever ways: "Why am I the only one ever to get punished? I have to go pee really bad!" Parents are encouraged to ignore these attempts at baiting during the brief time-out interval (most preschoolers require no more than 2 or 3 minutes, and school-age children 5 minutes for time-out to work).

Jack, a 10-year-old with ADHD, likes to annoy his two younger sisters. A typical day after school finds the three of them watching television while their mother prepares dinner in the adjacent kitchen, only to be frequently interrupted by complaints of Jack changing the television channel in midprogram or grabbing sisters' possessions. Relying on behavioral procedures, Jack's mother is quite directive, "Jack, you need to stay in your chair and keep hands to yourself. No channel changes without asking me first. If you do this, you can stay to watch television. If you touch your sisters or their things or change the channel, you will have a time-out."

Assuming Jack meets these expectations, he stays. If he violates them, he serves the time-out penalty (see Figure 8.11). Clearly this arrangement has some prospect of working because problem and target behaviors are both made clear and there are positive consequences for target behavior (access to television and sisters) and negative consequences for problem behavior (time-out and loss of access). If Jack were to require time-out, his mother could merely signal the consequence. Although difficult to do, parents should strive to remain calm and in control. Signs of anger, as reflected in facial expression or voice tone, may inadvertently signal to the child that they have upset the parent. In some instances, making parents angry is a desired consequence for the child. If so, a reaction from

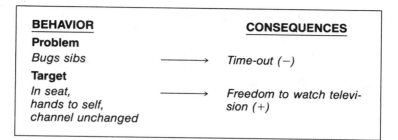

Figure 8.11. Use of time-out to promote compliance with parent's request ([−], negative consequence; [+], positive consequence).

Mom or Dad may only encourage the very behavior they are seeking to discourage.

Parents should also thus avoid much discussion after the time-out. Jack may feel quite unhappy about serving his 5 minutes in time-out, but this distress may be reduced if his mother goes into a lengthy discussion with him. Jack may see this as a good trade-off. Even though he had to endure a 5-minute time-out, the enjoyment of his individual time with mother offsets it. Time-out would then cease to be much of a negative consequence. By the same token, attempting to squeeze apologies or promises for future improvement out of the child often backfires. If the child has served the time, you have made your point. Drop it there.

Of course, many children refuse to go willingly to time-out, or refuse to stay, once there. This leaves parents with difficult choices. Young children or those who can be easily handled physically may do best if their parents escort them to time-out and hold them there if necessary. Tantrums may result and parents should be certain they are prepared to withstand the tantrum prior to taking physical action. Especially in the beginning, these tantrums can be long and violent. After it is clear that parents will insist on time-out no matter how severe the tantrum, then most children become increasingly willing to comply with time-out. Being held from behind while both parent and child are seated may be the best procedure. Besides controlling the child and avoiding injury to parent and child, this arrangement prevents eye contact with the child. Conversation should generally be withheld during this time.

One special word of warning is in order when considering time-out as a discipline procedure. There are exceptional children, most of them preschoolers with a history of moodiness, whose tantrums are so long and loud that they are virtually unable to quiet themselves. Assigning them to time-out may precipitate one of these unwanted tantrums. If your child has this degree of moodiness, then working with a professional to devise behavioral strategies, which may or may not include time-out, is essential.

Older and larger noncompliant children or teenagers present another challenge. This is especially true if the youngster has an explosive temper or is belligerent. Many parents state that they are unwilling or unable to coerce their children physically into time-out. After time-out is assigned and rejected, parents confront two unpleasant choices. One choice is simply to capitulate—that is, to drop the time-out demand and let life return to normal. For many, this is the poorer of the two choices. Another choice is to drop the subject in the short run, but bide time until the child can be induced to take the previously assigned time-out.

The scenario may be as follows: Lee, age 13 years, is told to take a time-out for swearing at his mother. He declines, and his mother is aware that she cannot force the issue physically. Rather than hounding Lee to comply, she immediately removes her attention, ceases eye contact, and suspends any verbal exchanges. Lee's initial reaction is a smile, perhaps assuming he can do as he wishes without consequences. After a few minutes, however, he approaches his mother with a question. Instead of answering, she forgoes eye contact and, in a soft tone, states, "After you have done your time-out I will talk with you." Lee scoffs and walks away. Later he again tries to initiate conversation but meets the same reaction from his mother. This time he angrily swears under his breath. His mother continues to ignore him, even though this taxes her self-control to the maximum. As the family's typical lunchtime approaches, he inquires about the offerings, only to be calmly reminded of the time-out that is due before lunch will be prepared for him. He swears loudly now. Again, his mother marshalls her power of self-control to ignore him. Finally, 2 hours after the first encounter, he requests a ride to a friend's house. When told the requirement is to serve time-out first, he grudgingly sits for 5 minutes in the square. After he does so, he is immediately taken to his friends without another word from his mother. Compliance with the time-out request is the target behavior at this point. His mother has provided him with a positive consequence promptly after he complied. For some extremely difficult children, getting them to take a time-out, even using difficult and lengthy steps like these, may be worth the effort. After the child complies with a time-out request once, subsequent compliance with time-out requests often becomes easier. This scenario may not always eventuate, but it represents a rational attempt to use consequences to work through a difficult discipline situation. Again, individual plans are best worked out with the help of a professional.

A final word about time-out is in order. Parents are encouraged to remember why time-out works—it is a consequence of boredom. Failures in the use of time-out often ignore this fact. "Ed, I want you to go take a bath now. If you don't get up and do it right away, then I will put you in time-out." Ed may well prefer time-out to the bathtub. If so, the intended negative consequence (isolation) turns out to be a positive consequence (a chance to be away from the bathtub). Parents must seek other strategies at that point. Perhaps telling Ed that he can continue to work on his model ship as soon as his bath is complete would work. Time-out can be an effective technique, but it has limitations. Trying to solve all behavior problems by applying time-out will fail.

Physical Prompt as a Negative Consequence

At times parents are unwilling to wait for time-out to work, and there may be an easier and more direct negative consequence. A physical prompt involves moving the child through the requested behavior by physical force, if necessary. For many children who enjoy resisting, this is an unpleasant prospect that either induces them to do what they were told or discourages future resistance.

Six-year-old Olivia becomes so wrapped up in her play that she often ignores her parents' directions to stop. Sometimes she defiantly responds, "No" or "In a minute" to directions. Her parents have tried to explain why they need prompt cooperation, but to no avail. When in an irritable mood, Olivia seems to enjoy dragging her feet and annoying her parents. Her mother, in particular, finds resistance infuriating. Time-out works sometimes, but it is not always viable. A mental health counselor encouraged Olivia's parents to try a physical prompt.

When Olivia, who was putting together a puzzle, ignored her mother's request to pick up her shoes and socks and join the family for dinner, a chance for a physical prompt arose (see Figure 8.12). Her mother told Olivia calmly, "Either pick up your shoes and socks and come to dinner now, or I will help you. If you do it on your own, I'll leave you alone." Olivia refused, her mother placed her hand on top of hers and "helped" her pick up the shoes and socks. She then nudged her to her room to deposit these items. Half way to her room Olivia pleaded, "I'll do it myself, just leave me alone," at which point her mother acquiesced by silently following behind her until she was seated at the table.

A physical prompt, even more than time-out, requires finesse. If parents become angry on the one hand, or are too accommodating in their help on the other, then the child may feel that their resistance is

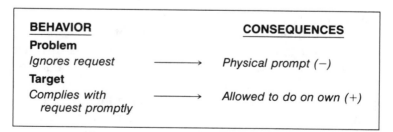

BEHAVIOR	CONSEQUENCES
Problem	
Ignores request ⟶	*Physical prompt (−)*
Target	
Complies with request promptly ⟶	*Allowed to do on own (+)*

Figure 8.12. Use of physical prompt to achieve compliance with parent's request to initiate an activity ([−], negative consequence; [+], positive consequence).

worth it. Of course, parents must never physically hurt the child or in any manner be abusive. The parent who learns to move the resisting child through the assigned activity rather assertively while conveying an attitude of "this is no inconvenience to me" often finds this technique invaluable. In contrast to time-out, this technique is generally of value only if used with younger children (8 years old or younger) and only if used rarely, no more than once or twice per day.

BEHAVIOR MANAGEMENT AS A WAY OF LIFE

Many parents' reaction to a suggested behavior management program is that it sounds like a great deal of effort and a great deal to remember, too. Is behavior management really practical? The answer is an emphatic yes!

Consider how much time you spend daily, as it is, disciplining your child. How much more work could it be to use behavioral principles? The biggest switch for parents who adopt behavioral techniques occurs *when* effort is expended, not how much. As parents we are apt to deal with problems after they arise. We scold or lecture in the hope of inducing change, or we simply vent frustration that things are going so badly. In contrast, a behavioral approach emphasizes creating a plan *before* the problem behavior has begun.

Recall the four questions that lead parents through the steps of behavior change (What problem behavior would I like to eliminate? What behavior would be more acceptable? What are the consequences of problem and target behaviors? How can I rearrange consequences to discourage problem and encourage target behavior?). If parents learn to ask themselves these questions when they anticipate problems, then many problems can be avoided. When a situation likely to result in a problem arises, the behaviorally astute parent creates a preventive plan. The children watching television in the next room, the family going for a car trip, or mealtime may signal to parents that it is time to make explicit expectations for positive behavior and to spell out positive and negative consequences. This "structure" maximizes chances for good behavior. For the child who anticipates consequences poorly (i.e., is impulsive), this outline is essential.

This type of arrangement has the enormous additional advantage of allowing parents to focus on success. By specifying target behavior, everyone is aware of what is expected and can notice when it has occurred. Rather than chiding for misbehavior, parents can praise for good behavior. Success can beget further success.

Many parents comment that they, too, learn new behaviors. Their use of behavioral techniques, especially outlining expectations and consequences, becomes second nature. These habits reach such an ingrained level that their use is no longer an effort. Only when new or difficult situations present themselves, must parents revert to careful, step-by-step development of a behavioral plan. If versed in behavioral strategies, most parents are quite capable of doing this. By working with a behavioral professional, of course, detailed plans and guidance can also be provided.

Remember, however, that the suggestions in this chapter are only the bare bones of behavior management. Professionals who work with children are familiar with behavioral techniques effective for a variety of unique problems ranging from aggression to lack of play skills. Such professionals can modify these techniques to fit your child and family circumstances as well as provide you with a framework and a general rationale for discipline. Recalling the warning that behavioral techniques do not alleviate attentional or hyperactivity problems, you may take heart that their judicious use can help maximize your child's development while making homelife more pleasant.

CONCLUSION

Because many children with ADHD have accompanying behavioral problems, parents are encouraged to learn techniques for behavior management. By learning to identify both problem behaviors and desired alternative behaviors, and by using consequences that promote behavioral change, parents can do much to help their children. The principles that are presented in this chapter thus comprise a foundation of knowledge upon which individual plans—specific to your child—can be developed with the help of a counselor or psychologist.

Chapter 9

Medication Treatment in ADHD

Martin Irwin

Use of medication to treat ADHD is controversial. Parents approach the use of medication—especially Ritalin, the most widely used medicine for ADHD—with extreme trepidation. You may have watched a television show, or read an article in the popular press, or been told by friends or relatives of the dangers of Ritalin. However, if you have read the scientific and medical literature on Ritalin, you can attest to the fact that there is a wide gulf between the public's misper-

---

In this chapter certain medications are identified by their brand name while others are identified by the generic name. Although it is usual in scientific literature to only use generic names, it was felt that when a brand name, such as Ritalin, is so familiar to the general population and the generic name of the same medication such as methylphenidate is much less recognizable, the brand name would be used. For medications whose brand names are not as commonly known to the average consumer, the preferred practice of using the generic name is followed.

ceptions and misinformation about this medication and the vast research findings showing that Ritalin and other similar stimulant medication, when used properly, are overall safe and effective.

How, then, did Ritalin earn its negative reputation? First, many children are placed on Ritalin without a thorough and comprehensive evaluation. Although Ritalin is an effective medication for ADHD, it is an inappropriate treatment for other disorders. Many children with other psychiatric disorders exhibit prominent although nonspecific symptoms of hyperactivity, distractibility, and impulsivity. When children receive only a cursory evaluation or no real evaluation at all, such underlying symptoms such as depression, suicidal thinking, paranoia, and other signs of psychopathology may be missed. These children may be mislabeled as having ADHD and inappropriately put on medication. Second, once a child is placed on medication, the medication needs to be monitored appropriately. Most primary care physicians, family practitioners, and pediatricians are familiar with the physical and medical side effects of Ritalin, but many of the side effects of this medication are not in this realm. Instead, they affect behavior, thinking, mood, and learning. The physician who monitors the medication must be familiar with the side effects in this area, as well as the specialized techniques (e.g., interviews and rating forms) to elicit appropriate information in this arena. The physician must also recognize the absolute necessity of obtaining information not only from the child and/or the parent but also from the school. With appropriate monitoring, side effects can be kept to a minimum and prevented from intensifying. Lastly, you as a parent need to be highly educated about these medications. As informed consumers, you can become empowered to help monitor the medication—finding the right dosage, recognizing early side effects, and avoiding serious side effects. You can thus enhance your child's overall treatment. Unfortunately, however, without thorough knowledge of the medication, parents may quickly become discouraged that the medication is not working or may become inappropriately alarmed at the appearance of a side effect they did not anticipate. This may lead to premature discontinuation of the medication. Avoiding the use of Ritalin or other medication due to fear, misperception, and misinformation denies the child optimal treatment. This chapter attempts to help parents make informed decisions and be knowledgeable consumers regarding medications for children with ADHD.

RITALIN

Action

Ritalin belongs to a class of medications known as stimulants. Other similar medications include Dexedrine, Cylert, and long-acting Ritalin or long-acting Dexedrine. The different stimulants have many similarities in action and in side effects. There are, however, some important differences, which are discussed later in this chapter.

Because of its overall high effectiveness, safety, and ease of use, Ritalin is typically the medication used first in the treatment of ADHD. Ritalin is a short-acting medication. It does not build up significantly in the blood stream. Rather, each dose almost stands alone. Because of this, multiple dosages must be given each day. Ritalin begins to work 20–40 minutes after it is taken. Its maximum effectiveness tends to occur within 1–1½ hours. After about 4 hours, it begins to wear off. There is variability in these times between children. But for any given child, once he or she has established a pattern, it tends to hold true.

Since the medication is so short acting, when starting the medication or changing the dose, a positive change should be apparent within 3–4 days. If there is no positive effect and there are no disabling side effects, the dosage can be increased every three to four days. A trial on a first stimulant (e.g., Ritalin) is likely to have a positive effect in approximately 70% of children. If unsuccessful, a trial on a second stimulant medication (e.g., Dexedrine) will increase the effectiveness of medication in up to 80%–85% of children.

When effective, Ritalin causes decreases in overactivity, in distractibility, and in impulsivity, resulting in an improvement in both behavior and short-term learning. For instance, a child who previously was unable to sit still and would get up and wander either at the dinner table or in the classroom may now be able to sit and complete a family dinner or classroom assignment. Similarly, a child who would be unable to follow through on tasks requiring multiple steps may now be able to complete chores at home, learn new material in school, and participate in group games and sports with peers. The child who would quickly, impulsively, and aggressively strike out at siblings, classmates, and peers may be able to slow himself or herself down and explore other more adaptive alternatives. Therefore, Ritalin may, in addition, result in improved parent-child relationships, peer relationships, and other important developmental tasks of childhood.

Although Ritalin and other stimulant medications are clearly effective, we do not know their exact neurochemical mechanism of action. However, it is unlikely that the stimulant effectiveness is paradoxical. A generation ago, it was taught that Ritalin has a paradoxical effect on children with ADHD. Whereas Ritalin would "stimulate" the non-ADHD child, it paradoxically would "calm" the "hyperactive" child. This is a myth. Stimulants increase alertness and on-task behavior while decreasing impulsivity and distractibility in most adults and children with or without ADHD. There are many examples of members of non-ADHD groups who respond to stimulants—such as college students during examinations or when tackling overdue term papers, or long-distance truck drivers. Such individuals might use stimulants to increase their alertness during periods when their usual level of arousal might be diminished but they must remain on task. (However, such misuse of stimulants, when not prescribed by a physician to a patient, is potentially dangerous. When used nontherapeutically, the dosage or even the chemical composition of the drug is not controlled, and serious side-effects or overdosage can frequently occur.) These examples illustrate that it is unlikely that stimulants reverse a dysfunction or biological deficit specific to ADHD children.

Side Effects

As with all medications, Ritalin does have side effects. The side effects need to be divided into those that are short term (i.e., appear immediately or within a few days of starting the medication or changing the dosage) or long term (i.e., appear long after a child is on a stable dose of medication).

Short-Term Effects

The short-term effects occur relatively frequently, but usually are not severe. Most children will experience some degree of appetite disturbance. They will report not being hungry, and/or some usually experience a mild sense of stomach upset. There may be some weight loss. It is important for parents to weigh their children weekly. For most children, some slight weight loss will not be a problem and will improve within 2–4 weeks. However, for the child who is already thin or if the weight loss persists, there are strategies available to help stabilize weight. For example, some or all of the medication doses can be given right after mealtime. Since the previous dose is wearing off, the child's appetite is less likely to be affected. The parent can also push high-caloric snacks. Although a child's appetite may be generally diminished, a child, even if not hungry, is still more likely to consume highly appealing foods. For the rare child where weight loss is of concern and cannot be reversed, the medication may need to be discontinued.

Another short-term side effect is sleep disturbance. Most children on Ritalin will have some difficulty falling asleep at their usual bedtime. Although the sleep disturbance is a direct biological side effect of the medication, the actual problems that result are not due to the medication per se, but to the resultant increased conflict between child and parents. Because many parents of ADHD children have been taught that predictability and structure are highly important, they may view a child's unwillingness to go to bed as part of a more general pattern of oppositional behavior found in ADHD children. The parents may thus insist on the child complying with an arbitrary bedtime. However, since the child is likely to be wide awake because of the effects of the medication, the child may refuse to go to bed. Bedtime then becomes a clash of wills between parents and child. Although the actual inability of the child to fall asleep at his or her usual bedtime cannot be avoided, the battles and conflict over bedtime can easily be avoided. It is important for parents to understand that the child is not being willful or oppositional. It is usually better to work out a program allowing the child to stay up quietly in his or her bedroom (or other room if the bedroom is shared with a sibling) until the child becomes tired and falls asleep, either reading, playing a quiet, solitary game, or listening to music. The insomnia is not a problem in and of itself. If the medication is having the desired therapeutic effect, even if the child gets less sleep at night, he or she should be fully alert and functioning the next day at school.

The third major and most problematic short-term side effect is known as rebound hyperactivity. Because the medication is short acting and does not build up to a steady state in the blood stream, each dose is an almost independent event accompanied by an on-off phenomenon. Thus, for many children, their functioning across the day is not smooth. Parents and teachers, and in many instances the children themselves, notice when the medication kicks in (turns on) and wears off. Early in the morning, in the interval after the preceding dose has begun to wear off and before the child has had the next dose of medication, and late in the day, the child's behavior is likely to be more variable. This may be most pronounced in children who receive the tradinal morning and lunchtime (two doses per day) medication regimen. These children will be essentially medication free throughout the late afternoon and evening hours. Many of these children will exhibit rebound hyperactivity, that is, their symptoms of hyperactivity, distractability, and impulsivity will reappear in the late afternoon and persist throughout the evening. For children with moderate to severe late-afternoon and evening rebound hyperactivity that does not improve after a few weeks, a third dose of medication in the late afternoon may be advisable. (The rationale and advantages for a three-dose-per-day schedule of Ritalin are discussed in detail later.) If the child is very sensitive to the on-off phenomenon of the medication and exhibits great difficulty early in the morning or in the interval between the last dose wearing off and the next dose kicking in, a change in timing of the medication may help. Although on average, each dose of medication lasts approximately 4 hours, for any given child the time interval might be significantly less. Therefore, some children require the medication at much shorter intervals; some children may need to receive their morning dose approximately a half hour before they fully wake up, get out of bed, and begin their day, so that they function better for morning routines; and some children may require multiple doses to help smooth out their functioning throughout the whole day. By adjusting the amount of medication, number of doses, and timing of doses, rebound hyperactivity can be avoided or minimized. Again, for the rare child where this does not happen, your physician may suggest that Ritalin be discontinued and an alternate medication attempted.

Increased irritability or mood change may also be associated with treatment on Ritalin. These symptoms are usually a result of the appetite disturbance, sleep disturbance, or rebound hyperactivity just discussed above. The irritability and mood change usually improve along with the course of the previously mentioned major side effects. However, if irritability and mood changes persist, did not preexist the initiation of medication, seem to be independent of the appetite or sleeping disturbance, are independent of the on-off phenomenon, and do not respond to the interventions outlined previously, the dosage of the medication may need to be decreased. If this does not help, medication eventually may need to be discontinued.

Lastly, if your child on Ritalin seems oversedated, overly focused, or overly slowed down, the medication may be at too high a dosage. Parents frequently describe this phenomenon as their child being like a "zombie." Almost invariably in such cases, the dosage of medication is too high. As a parent you should understand that children on an appropriate dosage of Ritalin should not seem overmedicated or in a stupor. Their overall personalities should still be recognizable. When this is not the case, the dosage of the medication, the appropriateness of the particular medication, and sometimes maybe even the correctness of the original diagnosis need to be questioned.

Long-Term Effects

Although most children will exhibit some degree of short-term side effects, there are a number of significant, although more rare, long-term side effects. With appropriate parental awareness and close physician monitoring, the long-term side effects should be recognized early and thus are easily reversible.

Decreased growth may be a side effect of stimulant medication. Although many studies have shown that children on stimulant medication achieve normal growth, some studies have reported growth retardation. Even when decreased growth occurs, however, it is usually not clinically significant for the individual child because the absolute amount of decreased growth is small. This is true even though research has shown that on the average those with and without Ritalin differ in growth, the difference in their growth is slight. For instance, a scientific study may report that a large number of children, say 1,000, who are taking Ritalin grow on average of one-quarter of an inch less than an equal number of children off medication. Although the absolute difference in height throughout the total period of growth is small and therefore is clinically insignificant to the individual child, the number of children in the two groups on and off medication is so large as to make the small difference of a quarter inch statistically significant. This results in parents becoming fearful that the medication will significantly stunt the growth of their child. However, this example illustrates how a statistically significant finding in large groups may be clinically insignificant to the individual children comprising the group. Once parents understand this, they need only take simple precautions against any significant growth stunting occurring in their child. It is advisable that all parents track their child's height every 3–4 months. They should mark their child's height against the same wall in a garage or other appropriate place in their home. In addition, they should have their child formally measured by their primary care physician at least yearly. Only in the rare cases, where the individual child is not gaining height anywhere near the expectations for his age, is it likely that the physician will stop the medication. In these children, soon after the discontinuation of the medication, their growth will usually resume at normal or accelerated rates, and within a matter of months they will catch up to where they should have been.

Tics (muscle twitches or abnormal motor movements) are another possible side effect of stimulant medication. Before being placed on medication, a child should be evaluated closely for the presence or family history of a tic disorder. If present, an alternative medication should be considered. If a child develops a tic while on stimulant medication, he or she should be monitored closely. Many tics in children are anxiety related, and most will disappear within days or weeks. However, if a tic persists for more than 2–3 weeks, the medication should probably be discontinued. If the child were to remain on the medication, there is a small chance that the tic might become irreversible and lead to a permanent tic disorder. On the other hand, if the tic is related to the use of the medication, the tic should be reversible upon stopping the medicine. There is one partial exception. Some children will experience increased eye blinking soon after beginning medication or a change in its dosage. This is likely different from the more pronounced and unusual motor movements that appear in much smaller numbers of children much later in treatment. Despite this, the eye blinking needs to be monitored. If the rate of eye blinking does not fall back to normal after 4–6 weeks, to avoid any chance that this might lead to a permanent disorder, the medication should probably be discontinued by your physician.

The last major long-term side effect of Ritalin can be the gradual emergence of paranoia. In overdosage, stimulant medication causes an acute paranoid reaction. Through a similar mechanism, about 2% of children who are treated long term with therapeutic doses of stimulant medication develop a paranoid reaction. Its onset, however, is very gradual and insidious. Often parents and even pediatricians notice that the child's personality is beginning to change, but because it is so gradual, they don't associate it with the child's usage of stimulant medication. Also, the symptoms occur around the time the child is entering adolescence, and therefore the symptoms are ascribed—as so many are in this age group—to puberty. It is important whenever parents suspect any change in their child's level of suspiciousness, fearfulness, or paranoia to report it as soon as possible. After further evaluation, if the symptoms are paranoia associated with the use of stimulant medication, the medication will probably be discontinued and the symptoms can be expected to gradually disappear. Although the paranoia associated with medication is reversible, it is important to recognize it early and to take appropriate action while the symptoms are still slight and not interfering overall with the child's day-to-day functioning.

Lastly, a number of phenomena have been labeled as side effects of Ritalin but in reality bear no direct connection to the taking of the medication. We live in an era where teenagers are at high risk for negative outcomes. About 15%–20% of all teenagers will suffer from suicidal behavior, drug or alcohol problems, and/or antisocial acts of violence. Clearly, with the rate of occurrence this high, many adolescents on Ritalin or similar medication will exhibit these difficulties. In many cases, when there is a bad outcome, the medication is blamed. Ritalin does not protect our youngsters against the difficulties that all teenagers experience. Likewise, it does not cause these difficulties. Well-executed research has documented that the adverse outcomes that all children are at risk for are not increased by the use of medication and therefore should not be blamed on use of the medication.

Finding the Appropriate Dosage

Ritalin is usually begun at a dosage of one pill (5 milligrams) twice a day, approximately 4 hours apart, usually in the morning and before lunch. The second dosage is generally given before lunch in order that it may already reach some degree of effectiveness by the time a child returns to the classroom after lunch. If appropriate feedback can be obtained from both the parents and the school teachers, the dosage can be raised in gradual increments of 2½–5 milligrams per dose every 3–4 days until gradual improvement is noted or troubling side effects have emerged. With younger children one may begin at an even lower starting dose and raise it much more gradually. With much older children and teenagers, physicians may begin at a higher dose and raise both doses simultaneously in somewhat larger increments. Once there is some improvement, the morning dose can be fine tuned by increasing it gradually in small increments until an optimal effect is obtained without an increase in side effects. This can again be done for the lunchtime dose. It is possible that the second dose may be slightly lower than the morning dose.

As mentioned previously, once the child is stabilized on a two-dose-per-day regimen, a decision should be made about the addition of a later afternoon third dose. Most children would benefit from this. It clearly helps children who have bad late-afternoon and evening rebound hyperactivity. In addition, most children with ADHD not only manifest dysfunctions at school but also have difficulties at home and with peer activities. Therefore, for many children, coverage with medication throughout the day is beneficial. This is especially crucial as the child gets a little older and experiences more demands around afterschool activities and homework. A third late-afternoon dose of Ritalin helps many of these children control their overactivity and impulsivity during peer activities and also concentrate and accomplish more while doing homework. Improved peer relationships and successful completion of homework are necessary for children to maintain their self-esteem and to be successful socially and academically. The younger child who can easily be managed behaviorally at home, who is not unsuccessful in many peer activities, and does not have much homework may be managed with only two doses per day. But for most children beyond fifth or sixth grade, the addition of a third dose can prove extremely helpful.

Medication-Free Holidays

Similar reasoning applies to the decision about whether to continue the medication on weekends and school and summer holidays. Since the vast majority of youngsters with ADHD have difficulties outside of school, they benefit from being on medication even when school is not in session. If the medication has any effect on a child's nonacademic functioning, it may be best to maintain him or her on the medication as consistently as possible. One of the tasks of childhood is for the youngster to begin to develop a sense of who he or she is. If a child is able to behave relatively consistently throughout the day and year, the process of identity formation is enhanced. However, if a child has one set of behaviors and personality traits while on the medication during the day and another set while off the medication (either in the evenings, weekends, or on holiday), that child experiences increasing confusion about his or her identity and may have difficulty integrating those two disparate parts of the self.

Discontinuing the Medication

For most children, the initial medication treatment should be for approximately $1\frac{1}{2}$–2 years. At that time, an attempt is often made to see if the child continues to need the medication. To truly determine whether a child still needs medication, the child must be kept medication free for approximately 4 weeks. Some children will exhibit a behavioral deterioration immediately following discontinuation of medication. This may occur because they feel different, both psychologically and physically, without the medication and are unused to this feeling. However, if given a few weeks, they may reach an equilibrium where they no longer need the medication. Therefore, if possible, the longer trial without medication is recommended. The usual procedure is to wean the child off medication during the summer when a deterioration in the child's behavior will be less detrimental and then have the child begin the school year without medication. Although on the surface this seems sensible, there are some problems with this approach. For the child whose behavior deteriorates and who will need to resume medication, beginning the school year badly and making a poor early impression on the teacher may negatively influence the whole course of the year, even once the child is back on medication. It may be better to wait until the middle of a school year when the child is learning optimally and already has established a good relationship with his or her teacher before discontinuing the medication. In the middle of the school year, the teacher can be engaged as an ally in helping to determine if a child can be maintained medication free. If the child does not do well off the medication, the teacher will have been made aware of all the steps in taking the child off the medication, will understand the reasons for the child's lessened functioning, and therefore will not change his or her overall opinion of the student. If the student needs to resume medication in this situation, most teachers will continue to maintain their positive regard for the student. From this position they can help the student overcome whatever negative factors were associated with the trial off the medication.

OTHER STIMULANTS

Dexedrine, another stimulant medication, is extremely similar to Ritalin. It has the same therapeutic effect and profile of side effects. However, there are salient differences. Although Dexedrine is also short acting, it is slightly longer acting on average than Ritalin, lasting approximately 5 hours instead of 4. Although this may be an advantage, on the other hand, Dexedrine is slightly more likely to cause the short-term, transient, although potentially annoying early side effects, and if they occur, they may be slightly more intense than those accompanying Ritalin. Therefore, on balance, Ritalin is the stimulant most physicians would first use with children 6 years of age and over. However, Ritalin is not recommended for use in children under 6. In children 3–5, the use of Dexedrine may be preferable.

One of the biggest disadvantages of Ritalin and Dexedrine is their short-acting nature. Therefore, three long-acting stimulants have been developed: Cylert, sustained-release Ritalin, and sustained-release Dexedrine. Of the three, Cylert is the most likely to be effective. Although there is some disagreement, the consensus among most of the research is that, in general, the long-acting stimulants are less likely to be effective than the short-acting regular Dexedrine or Ritalin, and even when effective, the long-acting preparations are less consistent in their effect. Therefore, in general, the use of regular Ritalin and Dexedrine is preferable. Cylert or the other long-acting stimulants are used most often in children who are unresponsive to the short-acting stimulants or in cases where it is impractical for the child to receive reliably the schooltime dose of medication (either because the child refuses to go to the nurse or there is no nurse available). In addition, Cylert has a side effect not reported with the other stimulants—liver toxicity. Although serious liver damage is rare, approximately 20% of children will have some rise in their liver enzymes.

TOLERANCE

For many children, at some point in the future after they have been on a steady and effective dose of stimulant medication, the medication seems to lose its effectiveness. This is called tolerance. Sometimes the development of tolerance occurs because the child was on the same dose for years during which the child's height and weight increased significantly. The former dose is simply no longer sufficient for the child's size. Other mechanisms of tolerance are less well understood. In all cases, the first intervention is usually to raise the dose of medication to determine if the higher dose will restore the earlier therapeutic effect. If a child is not having any side effects and is receiving appropriate monitoring for his medication, physicians often may cautiously raise the dose of medication even beyond what is recommended in the *Physicians' Desk Reference (PDR)* (standard reference guide to medication and its side effects). This is especially true for adolescents. It is a myth that Ritalin and other stimulant medications stop working at puberty. What typically happens with teenagers with ADHD is that the hyperactivity diminishes around puberty, but the distractibility and impulsivity remain unchecked. These teenagers often still require treatment with medication.

However, at the same time, it appears that their medication is no longer working. Again, this is usually owing to the fact that the dosage has remained unchanged for many years and with puberty and the accompanying growth spurts, the old dose is no longer effective. Since it is only recently that practitioners have become increasingly aware of the benefits of Ritalin during adolescence, it is necessary to treat many teenagers with what might appear to be relatively high doses of medication. Note, though, that the doses of Ritalin suggested in the *PDR* were formulated mainly for use in younger, school-age children and do not necessarily reflect the doses that much larger teenagers need to maintain clinical effectiveness.

At the same time, there are some children who develop tolerance to a given dosage very quickly. Every few months their dose needs to be increased. The interval between starting a new dose and the time that dose seems to lose its effectiveness becomes shorter and shorter. These children have become truly tolerant to the medication and may need to be placed on an alternative medication.

ALTERNATIVE MEDICATIONS

In addition to Ritalin and the other stimulants, two other major medications, each belonging to a different class of medications, have proven efficacy in treatment of ADHD. The drugs are Tofranil (imipramine), primarily used as an antidepressant, and clonidine, an agent used in treatment of high blood pressure. For the vast majority of children, stimulants (usually Ritalin) should be tried first. As previously discussed, they are highly effective, safe, and easy to use. However, in children with tics or a strong family history of movement disorder, or in those with prominent symptoms of paranoia and/or other psychotic-like symptoms or a strong family history of schizophrenia, use of stimulants may be contraindicated (medically inadvisable). It may be advisable to begin treatment with one of the alternatives first. In addition, when moderate symptoms of depression and/or anxiety coexist with the symptoms of ADHD, some experts would recommend starting imipramine first. However, if the depression and/or anxiety are not severe and these symptoms clearly seem to be a secondary reaction in a child who is always getting into trouble because of his impulsive behaviors, most experts would still recommend an initial trial on a stimulant. Some additional monitoring may be required, but stimulants may be worth a trial because of their high degree of effectiveness and safety.

Imipramine is a much more difficult medication to use. Although some results may be seen soon after initiating treatment, generally it takes 4–6 weeks to adjust the medication to the correct dose and to see optimal effectiveness. At too high a dose, imipramine can be a dangerous drug causing serious abnormalities in heart rhythm. However, the physician can and should take a number of precautions to ensure that a child does not develop these dangerous heartbeats. Before initiating treatment with an antidepressant, a careful medical history, physical examination, and electrocardiogram should be performed to ensure that the child has no preexisting cardiac disease. Then medication should be begun at a low dose and slowly raised in small increments. Periodically a blood level of the medication and a repeat cardiogram should be obtained to ensure that the level of medication in the bloodstream is not too high and that the child's heart rhythm has not changed (see Figure 9.1 for the protocol we use at the State

State University of New York
Health Science Center
Syracuse

Department of Psychiatry
and Behavioral Sciences
Division of Child and
Adolescent Psychiatry
(315) 473-8145

Imipramine is the treatment of choice for depression in childhood and a treatment for Attention Deficit Hyperactivity Disorder that is nonresponsive to stimulant medication. Before beginning the medication a baseline cardiogram, CBC, liver functions, kidney functions, thyroid functions, and fasting blood sugar should be obtained. The medication should be begun at 25 mg bid (50 mg hs in older children) and if well tolerated increased quickly to 1½ mg per kilogram per day in three divided dosages (two doses per day in older children). After 6 days, an imipramine blood level drawn before the morning medication and a repeat EKG should be obtained.

If the blood level is below the therapeutic level and the cardiogram shows no signs of toxicity, the imipramine dose should be increased by 25 mg every 3 to 4 days as tolerated until the dosage reaches 3 mg per kilogram per day in three divided doses. Approximately 1 week later, a repeat imipramine blood level and cardiogram should again be obtained before the morning medication.

In EKG monitoring, the limits are:

PR interval: less than or equal to 0.21 seconds
QRS interval: widening to no more than 30% over baseline QRS interval
Heart rate: no more than 130 beats/minute
Systolic pressure: no more than 130 mmHg
Diastolic pressure: no more than 85 mmHg

If the blood level is still below the therapeutic level and the cardiogram shows no signs of toxicity, the imipramine dose should be increased by 25 mg every 3 to 4 days as tolerated until the dosage reaches 5 mg per kilogram per day in three divided doses. Approximately 1 week later, a repeat imipramine blood level and cardiogram should be obtained. If there are still no signs of toxicity, the patient should be maintained at that dosage.

I would like to have the patient return for a follow up visit 2–4 weeks after he or she has been on a dosage of imipramine at therapeutic blood level or 5 mg per kilogram.

Please call me at any time if you have questions about the patient or the administration and monitoring of this protocol.

Martin Irwin, M.D.
Director, Division of Child
  and Adolescent Psychiatry
Associate Professor of Psychiatry
  and Pediatrics

Committed to Excellence in Professional Education, Patient Care and Research.

College of Medicine   College of Graduate Studies   College of Health Related Professions   College of Nursing
University Hospital
750 East Adams Street, Syracuse, N.Y. 13210

Figure 9.1. Protocol for use of imipramine to treat ADHD, used by State University of New York Health Science Center, Syracuse.

University of New York Health Science Center). With these precautions, imipramine can be used safely. However, the repeated trips to the laboratory for blood tests and to the doctor's office or hospital for cardiograms make the use of this drug much more difficult and costly than treatment with Ritalin. In addition to potential problems with heart rhythm, imipramine has a number of other, less dangerous side effects. Imipramine is somewhat sedating. It can cause dizziness and a drop in blood pressure when there is a sudden change in position, such as quickly going from lying down to standing up. It is constipating. It can also cause dry mouth, blurred vision, increased sweating, and some other annoying symptoms. Generally, these side effects are short lived and are tolerated very well, especially by children. Imipramine should be used very cautiously in children where there is a suspicion of seizures or if a child is already taking antiseizure medication. In addition, care should be taken when combining imipramine with certain cold preparations, asthma medications, and others. This should be discussed thoroughly with your pediatrician.

When used in large groups of children, imipramine may be slightly less effective (effective in a slightly smaller number of children) than the stimulants. However, when effective, the drug provides some potential advantages. First, imipramine offers a much smoother mode of action than the stimulants. There is no pronounced rebound or on-off phenomenon. Second, because the drug builds up in the bloodstream to a steady state, the exact timing of dosages is not crucial and there is no major problem if a dose is occasionally overlooked. In addition, children on imipramine tend to have improved sleep patterns. Therefore, imipramine may be especially indicated for ADHD children who have had extreme preexisting nighttime difficulties or have developed serious sleep difficulties secondary to treatment with stimulants.

Clonidine, the second major drug previously mentioned, is an antihypertension drug with some proven efficacy in treating ADHD. Clonidine may be especially effective in children with ADHD who also have prominent symptoms of overarousal, anger, and aggression. In addition, Clonidine is an effective treatment for Tourette's syndrome (multiple tic disorder). However, it is a highly sedating drug that can cause significant drops in blood pressure. Because of these two side effects, the dosage of clonidine must be increased extremely slowly so that the child does not become overwhelmed. Because of these side effects, clonidine would not generally be considered a drug of first choice except possibly in children who suffer from ADHD symptoms plus tics and/or have a strong family history of tic disorders. Clonidine may also be indicated for children with ADHD who exhibit significant overarousal, anger, and/or aggression who did not adequately improve with treatment or stimulants.

Other possible treatments for ADHD, such as propranolol, lithium, Prozac, and others are much more experimental and less proven. Generally, they should be used only after all standard treatments have failed.

DECIDING TO CHANGE MEDICATION

In some children who have not responded to the first medication, a second medication will need to be tried. These children may have been overwhelmed by side effects with the first medication, or after a period of time they may have developed true tolerance to it. The usual procedure in children who began using a stimulant would be to try a different stimulant medication.

Although all stimulants have similar therapeutic effects and similar profiles of side effects, an individual child may get a good therapeutic response on a trial of a second stimulant where he or she did not respond to the first stimulant. That is, Dexedrine may be tried even if the child did not have a beneficial response to Ritalin. Similarly, although overall the side effects are similar, any given child may experience different side effects on two different medications in the same class. For instance, some youngsters exhibit excellent therapeutic response to the initial stimulant medication, only to develop serious difficulties maintaining appropriate weight or growth, necessitating discontinuation of the initial medication. When switched to a different stimulant, most of these children continued to maintain the positive therapeutic gains but did not develop the accompanying weight or growth disturbances. There are, however, some exceptions to this general recommendation. If the side effect to the first stimulant is either tics or paranoia, it is probably ill-advised to attempt treatment with a second stimulant; an alternative medication treatment should be considered. In addition, if a child with co-existing depression and/or anxiety did not receive an adequate initial response to the first stimulant, it would probably be more effective to initiate a second medication trial with imipramine instead of a second stimulant. Similarly, in a youngster who exhibits minimal distractibility but much more prominent symptoms of impulsive behavior and has failed a trial on stimulant medication, it may be advisable to proceed directly to a trial on Clonidine.

CONCLUSION

The use of medication to treat children with ADHD can be highly effective. If you as a parent understand the different choices of medication, indications and guidelines for their use, potential side effects, and the need for appropriate monitoring, you can become an important partner in making informed treatment decisions about your child. You can help guarantee that your child will receive rational and optimal treatment—free of myths and misinformation—that can make a significant, positive difference in his or her life.

Chapter 10

ADHD and Eligibility for Special School Services

with Robert R. Davila

Because ADHD[1] has broad implications for classroom learning, the Office of Special Education and Rehabilitative Services, the Office for Civil Rights, and the Office of Elementary and Secondary Education within the U.S. Department of Education have recently clarified state and local responsibility under federal law for addressing the school needs of children with ADHD. As the parent of a student diagnosed with ADHD or one who is suspected of having ADHD, you are encouraged to learn as much as possible about the rights of students with disabilities and particularly about the rights of children with ADHD. This chapter

---

[1]Although we recognize the differing definitions of ADHD and ADD (attention deficit disorder), and although federal documents frequently refer to ADD, for the sake of consistency within this book, the acronym ADHD is used throughout this chapter to encompass both disorders.

summarizes the current position of the Department of Education on educating students with ADHD. Federal law represents a minimum guarantee of student rights, although state laws and regulations may offer greater rights to students and parents.

ELIGIBILITY FOR SPECIAL EDUCATION AND RELATED SERVICES

The Individuals with Disabilities Education Act (IDEA, PL 101-476), formerly the Education of the Handicapped Act, authorizes and funds special education services. In 1990, during the reauthorization of the IDEA, the U.S. Congress seriously considered including ADHD in the definition of "children with disabilities." Had they done so, ADHD would have become a separate disability category. This change would have made students with ADHD eligible for services under the IDEA by virtue of their disorder, just as children with other disabilities, such as learning disabilities or hearing impairments, are eligible if they are determined to be in need of special education and related services. However, since many students with ADHD are readily able to qualify for services under the IDEA without creation of a separate category (as discussed later in this chapter), the Department of Education took the position that there was no need to create a new and separate category for ADHD.

Although no change was thus made in the categories of children eligible for services, the Secretary of Education was required by Congress to solicit public comment on special education for children with ADHD. The department subsequently received over 2,000 written comments. The comments indicated that confusion existed in the field regarding the extent to which students with ADHD may be served in special education programs under the IDEA. As a parent, you may have experienced some of this confusion.

Services Afforded under IDEA

For children with disabilities who are found eligible for special education and related services under the IDEA, the law provides that a "free appropriate public education" be provided. That is, special education instruction and related services, such as counseling, are provided at no cost to parents. The actual services that are provided must be spelled out in an individualized education program (IEP) for each child. This is a plan that details which special education and related services will be provided by which instruction personnel and how progress toward each student's educational goals will be measured. The law also provides that various rights and protections, such as the right to an independent evaluation and the right for parent input into the student's education plan, be extended to children with disabilities and their parents.

To be eligible under the IDEA, a student must undergo an evaluation and be found to have one or more of the 13 disabilities specified in the IDEA. The student must also be in need of special education and related services. It is the responsibility of state education agencies and local school districts to provide special education and related services to children with ADHD who are determined to have one of the special-education-eligible disabilities (discussed in the sections following) and to be in need of special education and related services (see Table 10.1). These services must meet each child's unique educational needs. Services must include those required to meet needs arising from the

Table 10.1. Key terms in qualifying children with ADHD for school services

IDEA: Individuals with Disabilities Education Act. Formerly the Education of the Handicapped Act, this federal law governs special education services.

Learning Disabilities: One of the 13 categories of disability for which students may qualify for special education under the IDEA. In many states students are identified by a severe discrepancy between IQ and academic achievement. Accompanying problems, such as memory or perception, are required in some states.

Seriously Emotionally Disturbed: One of the 13 categories of disability for which students may qualify for special services under the IDEA. Students are usually identified by longstanding problems of mood, interpersonal relationships, anxiety, thinking, or behavior that prevent school progress.

Other Health Impaired: One of the 13 categories of disability for which students may qualify for special education services under the IDEA. Students with ADHD may qualify for services if their problem is deemed a chronic or acute health problem that "results in limited alertness adversely affecting educational performance."

Section 504 (of the Rehabilitation Act of 1973): This is a non–special education method of providing services to students with disabilities. Some students receive services if ADHD is viewed as a "physical or mental impairment which substantially limits a major life activity."

ADHD condition. A full continuum of alternative placements must be available, including instruction in regular classes, special classes, and special schools; home instruction; and instruction in hospitals and institutions. The IDEA requires that students be educated in the least restrictive environment that meets their needs. The sections following discuss several of the disability categories into which children with ADHD often fall.

Eligibility for Special Education by Virtue of Learning Disability

One of the categories of disabilities under which students with ADHD may be found eligible for special education services is learning disabilities. It is known that children with ADHD have a substantially higher rate of learning disabilities than children without ADHD. Just like children without ADHD, those with ADHD must satisfy the criteria for learning disabilities if they are to receive this designation and are to be afforded special education and related services. The federal definition of a specific learning disability is:

> [A] disorder in one or more of the basic psychological processes involved in understanding or in using language, spoken or written, that may manifest itself in an imperfect ability to listen, think, read, write, spell, or do mathematical calculations. The term (learning disabilities) includes such conditions as perceptual disabilities, brain injury, minimal brain dysfunction, dyslexia, and developmental aphasia. The term does not apply to children who have learning problems that are primarily the result of visual, hearing, or motor disabilities, of mental retardation, of emotional disturbance, or of environmental, cultural, or economic disadvantage. (PL 102-119, 20 USC 1401[a][1])

This definition was clarified by additional federal regulations. These regulations specify that children qualify as having learning disabilities only if certain conditions are met. Practically speaking, a learning disability designation is possible only if the child does not achieve commensurate with his or her peers in one or more of the following areas, *and* a significant discrepancy exists between a student's ability and his or her achievement in at least one of the following areas:

Oral expression
Listening comprehension
Written expression
Basic reading skill
Reading comprehension

Mathematics calculation
Mathematics reasoning

Testing and evaluation of the child suspected of having a learning disability are often performed by a school psychologist and are termed a psychoeducational evaluation. However, some states require or encourage other forms of testing and evaluation that assist both in determining whether that child has a learning disability and also in developing a program to meet the child's needs. Findings from the child's evaluation are among the sources of information that a multidisciplinary team uses to decide on eligibility for services under the IDEA.

Eligibility for Special Education by Virtue of Serious Emotional Disturbance

Another category under which students with ADHD may qualify for special education services is serious emotional disturbance. Here, too, students with ADHD must meet the established criteria. They neither automatically qualify nor are they automatically disqualified for services because they have ADHD. The federal definition for serious emotional disturbance is as follows:

> The term means a condition exhibiting one or more of the following characteristics over a long period of time and to a marked degree that adversely affects a child's educational performance:
>
> 1. An inability to learn which cannot be explained by intellectual, sensory, or health factors;
> 2. An inability to build or maintain satisfactory interpersonal relationships with peers and teachers;
> 3. Inappropriate types of behavior or feelings under normal circumstances;

4. A general pervasive mood of unhappiness or depression;

5. A tendency to develop physical symptoms or fears associated with personal or school problems.

The term includes schizophrenia. The term does not apply to children who are socially maladjusted, unless it is determined that they have a serious emotional disturbance. (PL 102-119, 20 USC 1401[a][1])

To be identified as having a disability in this category, students must exhibit one of the five preceding characteristics to a marked degree, the problem must have been evident for a substantial time period, and the problem must affect educational performance. Some, but not all, children with ADHD meet these criteria.

Eligibility for Special Education by Virtue of "Other Health Impaired" Category

"Other health impaired" is another one of the 13 disability categories under which students with ADHD may qualify for special education services. Many health problems can potentially create eligibility for special services under this category. There is no exhaustive list, but among its provisions, the term *other health impaired* includes all chronic and acute impairments that result in limited alertness that adversely affects educational performance. If a student with ADHD has a chronic (meaning *longstanding*) or acute (meaning *of recent onset*) health problem (ADHD itself may be considered to be a health problem) that results in limited alertness (e.g., poor attention to classroom instruction), then he or she may be considered disabled and eligible for special education services solely on the basis of the ADHD impairment. That is, a child with ADHD may be eligible under the "other health impaired" category without having evidence of learning disabilities or serious emotional disturbance. Again, the student must meet the criteria to be eligible for services. The mere diagnosis of ADHD is insufficient to create special education eligibility.

EVALUATIONS FOR
SPECIAL EDUCATION SERVICES

State education agencies and local school districts have an affirmative obligation to evaluate children suspected of having any of the disabilities discussed thus far. The IDEA requires state agencies and local school districts to have procedures for locating, identifying, and evaluating all children suspected of having a disability and who are in need of special education and related services. This responsibility is known as "child find." It is applicable to all children from birth to 21 years of age, regardless of the severity of their disability.

The obligation to identify students with disabilities includes the requirement that evaluations of children suspected of needing special education and related services be conducted without undue delay. There are other requirements as well. Local school districts may not refuse to evaluate a child for special services who has a prior medical diagnosis of ADHD solely because of that diagnosis. Thus, a local school district cannot refuse to evaluate a child's eligibility for services merely because a physician has already indicated that the child has ADHD. Another point is equally important. *A medical diagnosis of ADHD alone is insufficient to render a child eligible for special education services.* Thus, a physician's statement that a child has ADHD does not create automatic eligibility. The student still must be found eligible by meeting the criteria for one or more of the special education categories and have a demonstrated need for specially designed instruction.

The IDEA spells out the required sequence of events for a child to receive special education and related services. To begin, a full, individualized evaluation of the child's educational needs must be conducted prior to placement in a special education program or related services. This evaluation must be conducted by a multidisciplinary team (i.e., professionals from various disciplines such as education, psychology, medicine, or nursing). The evaluation team must include at least one teacher or other specialist with knowledge in the suspected disability.

Disagreements sometimes arise over evaluations, and the IDEA also addresses these concerns. If a parent disagrees with the local school district's refusal to evaluate a student or with the school district's determination that a student does not have a disability (i.e., is not eligible for special education services), then remedies are available. These remedies include an important parental right, the right to request a due process hearing. The due process hearing offers a chance for parents to present their concerns, for the local school district to make its position clear, and for a binding opinion to be rendered by an independent hearing officer.

SECTION 504
OF THE REHABILITATION ACT OF 1973

The preceding discussion indicates that some students with ADHD will not qualify for special education and related services according to the IDEA. Important alternatives may nonetheless exist for these students. Section 504 of the Rehabilitation Act of 1973 and its implementing regulations may be applicable in these instances. Section 504 prohibits discrimination on the basis of disability by recipients of federal funds. Most public schools in the United States receive some federal funds. Since Section 504 is a civil rights law rather than a funding law, its requirements are framed in different terms than those of the IDEA. Although the Section 504 regulation was written with an eye to consistency with the IDEA, it is more general, and there are some important differences. One crucial difference is that some children who are determined to have a disability under Section 504 may be afforded protection under Section 504 but may not be eligible for special education under one of the disability categories under the IDEA.

Definition of Disability in Section 504

Section 504 requires every recipient operating a public elementary or secondary education program to address the needs of children with disabilities under Section 504. Students with disabilities must have their needs met as adequately as the needs of students without disabilities. The definition of "person with a disability" is thus crucial. As defined in the Section 504 regulation, a "person with a disability" is any person who has a physical or mental impairment substantially limiting a major life activity such as learning, has a record of such an impairment, or is regarded as having such an impairment. Thus, depending on the severity of their condition, children with ADHD may fit within that definition.

Programs and Services under Section 504

Under Section 504, a local school district must provide a free appropriate public education to each qualified child with a disability. In this sense, children identified under Section 504 and the IDEA are offered similar basic guarantees. A free appropriate public education, under Section 504, consists of regular or special education and related aids and services. These must match the individual student's needs. Under Section 504, if there is reason to believe that a child has ADHD and is in need of special education and related services, the local school district must evaluate the child to determine if he or she is "disabled" according to Section 504. If the local school district determines that the child is not "disabled" under Section 504, the parent has the right to contest that determination. On the other hand, if the child is found to be "disabled" under 504, steps will be taken to aid the student. The local school district then determines the child's educational needs. Regular or special education services might be offered, or related aids or services alone may be found sufficient. An IEP developed in accordance with the IDEA is one means of meeting the free appropriate public education requirement of Section 504, but a formal IEP document is not mandated by Section 504.

As is true under the IDEA, the child's education must be provided in the educational mainstream to the maximum extent appropriate. For example, students eligible under Section 504 are to be educated in the regular classroom, unless it is demonstrated that education in this setting would not be appropriate even with the use of supplementary aids and services. By the same token, should it be determined that the student with ADHD is "disabled" under Section 504 but needs only modifications in the regular learning environment, then these adjustments are required by Section 504. In such a case it would be impermissible to remove the child from the regular classroom. Regular classroom teachers are important in identifying appropriate education adaptations and interventions for many students with ADHD. Chapter 12 of this book discusses a number of interventions that can occur within the child's classroom without extensive support or elaborate aids.

State educational agencies and local school districts have been encouraged by the federal government to take steps to coordinate their services under IDEA and Section 504. Similarly, they have been encouraged to train regular education teachers and other school personnel. The goal is first to enhance awareness among school personnel about ADHD and its manifestations, and, second, to provide for the adaptations that can be implemented in regular programs to address the instructional needs of students with ADHD.

The types of interventions that are expected to be implemented under Section 504 were made clear in a September 16, 1991, memorandum from the U.S. Department of Education that suggests the following:

> providing a structured learning environment: repeating and simplifying instructions about in-class and homework assignments; supplementing verbal instructions with visual instructions; using behavioral management techniques; adjusting class schedules; modifying test delivery; using tape recorders, computer-aided instruction and other audio-visual equipment; selecting modified textbooks or workbooks; and tailoring homework assignments.

Other ways to meet special needs have been identified by the federal government as well. These range from consultation services to special resources and may include reducing class size; use of one-on-one tutorials; classroom aides and note takers; involvement of a "service coordinator" to oversee implementation of special programs and services, and possible modifications of nonacademic times such as lunchroom, recess, and physical education. It is believed that through adaptations and interventions in the regular classroom, many of which may be required by Section 504, local school districts will be able to provide effective instruction for many students with ADHD.

Procedural Safeguards of Students' Rights under Section 504

Procedures to protect the rights of students and parents are included under Section 504; they are, however, less specific than those under the IDEA. The Section 504 regulations require local school districts to make available a system of procedural safeguards. These safeguards permit parents to challenge actions regarding identification, evaluation, or educational placement of their child with a disability who they believe needs special education or related services. Safeguards under Section 504 include notification of programs and placement decisions, an opportunity for parents to examine records, an impartial hearing with opportunity for parental participation and representation by counsel, and a review procedure. School districts and state education agencies may use the same due process procedures for resolving disputes under both the IDEA and Section 504, but a separate procedure can also be used under Section 504.

CONCLUSION

It is important for parents and school personnel to understand the laws and regulations regarding the education of children with ADHD. Congress and the Department of Education agree. They have recognized the need to provide information and assistance for teachers, administrators, parents, and other interested persons regarding the identification, evaluation, and instruction of children with ADHD. The Department of Education is forming links with education associations to consider cooperatively programs and services needed by children with ADHD across the spectrum of regular and special education. In addition, six federal research centers are working with state and local educational agencies to identify effective evaluation and intervention procedures being implemented around the country. Moreover, the 10 regional offices of the Office for Civil Rights will provide technical assistance to parents and educators. The Office of Special Education and Rehabilitative Services is furthermore funding four additional centers to synthesize existing research knowledge in assessment and interventions for meeting the needs of children with ADHD. Eventually the office will be funding projects to train school administrators and teachers about the needs of such children and effective identification and intervention strategies. The Federal Resource Center located at the University of Kentucky is also identifying successful practices and programs for serving students with ADHD at the local level.

Increased awareness of the unique educational needs of children with ADHD has prompted action by educators, parents, and federal agencies. Working together, these groups can help assure a promising future for students with ADHD.

Chapter 11

Finding the Best School Placement

Among the foremost concerns expressed by parents is where to educate their child with ADHD. This concern is justified based on findings that an estimated 23%–30% of children with ADHD have problems achieving at the level predicted by their IQ scores, and that between 30% and 70% of children with ADHD have failed at least 1 year of school. Without an appropriate educational program, many such children will drop out of school. Finding the right educational setting is thus crucial.

REGULAR PUBLIC SCHOOL CLASS PLACEMENT—NO SPECIAL DESIGNATION

As Chapter 10 suggested, services for many children with ADHD can be provided in the public school, many of these in your child's regular classroom, and often with no labels involved. You are encouraged to consider this option first, because with no labels there is no stigma, and provided your child's needs can be adequately met, the child experiences little or no negative impact. However, this option requires teachers to do what is necessary even though no formal label of ADHD is involved, no special funding occurs, and administrative support may not be offered. If a viable plan is feasible under these conditions, fine. Labeling in itself has no special value, so long as the child's condition is understood and his or her needs are fulfilled. Many experienced teachers can individualize so that the child with ADHD succeeds, especially if other aspects of the child's life are successful. Other teachers find that by working with a school psychologist or school counselor, or alternatively with an out-of-school professional, a fairly straightforward plan can be devised and implemented. The plan is not sufficiently unique that other labels or special designations are called for; both parents and teachers are satisfied to leave things on an informal basis.

ASSISTANCE IN THE
REGULAR CLASS UNDER SECTION 504

The next chapter discusses some of the many techniques that can be used to help children with ADHD in a regular classroom. Implementing these techniques may require special support or assistance, however. Often, the local school district must concur with the ADHD diagnosis and sanction an individualized plan if the child's needs are to be met. By invoking Section 504 of the Rehabilitation Act of 1973, the school is required to provide necessary support personnel or modifications, but the child is not identified as a special education student, and no special education labels are entered into his or her school records. Recall that under Section 504 programming changes may be made, but only the ADHD label is used. A program authorized by Section 504 may be an excellent compromise because the child receives a minimum of stigmatizing labels but may receive substantial services.

RESOURCE
SPECIAL EDUCATION ASSISTANCE

Another variant of leaving the child in his or her regular classroom is to use "resource" special education services, if the child qualifies. Many students with ADHD will quality for special education services in the categories of learning disabilities, serious emotional disturbance, or "other health impaired," as discussed in the preceding chapter. For those who do, a "resource" special education placement may be the best choice. With this arrangement, as with the nonspecial education option just mentioned, the student remains primarily in the general education classroom. However, a special education teacher provides direct tutoring or instructional services, and assists the regular teacher by securing distinctive materials or by arranging novel teaching methods, or both. Access to trained special education personnel, formal designation as a student with special needs, and yet the chance to receive services in the context of the regular class make this option hard to beat for many students. As emphasized in Chapters 10 and 12 in this book, extensive services can be delivered in such an arrangement; no preexisting limit on amount or character of resource services exists.

Unfortunately, many students who could potentially benefit from resource special education services are denied them because of lack of eligibility. Teachers and parents are thus left to work out acceptable programs via Section 504 protections or solely by relying on the goodwill of the school.

SELF-CONTAINED
SPECIAL EDUCATION PLACEMENT

Some special education—eligible students require more than resource assistance. If this is the case, the next option to be considered is a self-contained classroom. This is an ungraded class, usually consisting of no more than 12 students and a special education teacher. Often, one or more aides is also available. The advantages here are obvious. Individualized instruction is possible, the teacher-to-student ratio is maximized, and exotic programming, such as using a classwide token economy assigning points for acceptable behavior and trading those points for rewards, is feasible. Students benefit from an uninterrupted day's instruction by the same teacher(s), thus maximizing detection and implementation of the best and most individualized teaching methods.

This is a costly option for the school district, and it has the disadvantage of segregating children with problems from their peers. This latter fact can be stigmatizing. It may also preclude the chance for children with ADHD to learn more acceptable behavior by depriving them of exposure to suitable peer models. For these reasons, relatively few children are placed in self-contained special education classes. Those that are typically have failed in the regular classroom, even with considerable resource assistance.

SPECIAL EDUCATION SCHOOL AND
RESIDENTIAL SCHOOL PLACEMENT

A very few children with ADHD cannot be successfully educated in a self-contained classroom located on the campus of a public school. Of this group, some will attend classes in quite specialized, off-campus special schools. Large districts might manage their own schools of this type: a 30-student school for children with serious emotional disturbance is an example. Contracting with a private special education school is another option. Some students' problems are so formidable that residence on the campus of a special school, where class is attended during the day, is mandatory. This residential option is the most restrictive and extreme of those discussed here. Some districts have never planned or implemented such a placement, and do not anticipate doing so in the future.

Children who require such a stringent placement usually have several severe problems (i.e., ADHD and severe conduct disorder). The severity of ADHD alone is almost never sufficient to prompt such a placement. As a parent, you would generally be advised to seek this option only if all else has failed. The advantages of extreme control, individualization of treatment, and staff expertise are generally negated by the disruption in the child's normal education and social life. Of course, for the child who would be incapable of receiving an education elsewhere, this option is acceptable.

VALUE AND LIMITATIONS OF SPECIAL EDUCATION SERVICES

Special education services (whether resource, self-contained, or special school setting) are of immense value. For many children, they make the difference between school failure and success, between happiness and satisfaction and sadness and despair. Without special education services many children would learn little; many would drop out of school at the earliest opportunity.

The fact that services are provided without expense to parents is an obvious and important advantage. The cost to the public school of providing for one child can easily be several thousand dollars a year. Participation in special education also means that certified, professionally qualified teachers are providing services. Moreover, there are obvious legal safeguards for your child. For example, each child must be placed in the least restrictive environment, a provision requiring that schools consider an array of services, from the simple and nonintrusive to the complex and potentially intrusive, for each child.

PRIVATE (REGULAR) SCHOOL PLACEMENT

A common reaction of parents upon learning of the ADHD diagnosis is to seek a private school so that their child can be better educated. The desire for more individualized, or what is perceived as more compassionate, instruction is often the motivation for a private setting. However, although some private schools' favorable teacher-to-student ratios and their commitment to children make for a good placement, often such placements are a poor idea, for several reasons.

Many private schools have neither the resources nor the desire to educate children with ADHD. Teachers in private schools may know less about learning difficulties and behavior and attention problems than public school teachers. Private schools, by their definition, do not serve all students, as public schools do. Accordingly, they may lack techniques for individualizing instruction and the know-how to encourage acceptable behavior. Even when individual accommodations are possible, private schools may balk at the requisite staffing demands and the diversion of teaching time away from their other students. Thus, some private schools exclude students with ADHD.

A candid discussion of your child's needs and a dispassionate appraisal of the school's ability to meet them is advised before agreeing to a private school placement. You may want to ask pointed questions about other students with ADHD who have enrolled, or request to view examples of programs worked out for them. At any rate, a healthy skepticism backed by an insistence on facts is suggested.

PRIVATE SPECIAL SCHOOL PLACEMENT

The rare private school organized specifically for children with learning, behavior, or attention problems may offer the same advantages, as the special education schools discussed earlier. In some exceptional instances, such a school may offer unique advantages too. For instance, a special school located at a university or medical school might link treatment with the latest research findings or have knowledgeable experts on hand to contribute to the program.

For private special schools that lack these valuable but uncommon pluses, there are unfortunate disadvantages compared to their public education special school counterparts. These revolve around finances. It is difficult for programs supported solely by tuition from parents (and perhaps endowment) to compete for professional staff with public-supported schools. Thus, a private setting often cannot attract or retain quality teachers or garner the necessary funds for building improvement, materials, and supplies. This is so because any program devoted to special students must have an extremely rich teacher-to-student ratio; these are expensive programs to run. Although local factors vary, generally public education's access to federal and state money makes it more favorable than private programs. Often parents are better served by working with the public school by explaining their child's unique needs rather than exercising the private option. At times, of course, considerable lobbying is called for, and outside professionals may need to be called on to explain the rationale for more services.

MILITARY AND STRUCTURED BOARDING SCHOOLS

Structure, consisting of clear expectations and consequences to back up those expectations, has already been said to benefit many children with ADHD. So does a predictable daily routine. Some live-in programs devoted exclusively to caring for children and teenagers can provide a degree of structure unattainable at home. Military schools and boarding schools with carefully planned patterns of daily activities are examples of placements that sometimes help children or teenagers with ADHD.

Military schools have a reputation for imposing discipline and structure on their student body. Military schools promote an obvious code of conduct, they typically impose group and individual consequences for not adhering to that code, and students' days are usually filled with organized activities so that there is little free time. Moreover, an organizational plan that places individuals into prearranged groups or units may, for some, provide an otherwise difficult-to-obtain chance for acceptance. Some children may develop a sense of pride and competence here that had eluded them elsewhere.

The risk for this type of arrangement, however, is inflexibility. Rules that are too rigid to accommodate individual differences (e.g., the student unable to sustain attention on long tasks) may cause some to fail unnecessarily. Children with coexisting conduct or oppositional problems (see Chapter 1) may also encounter recurrent conflict with authority. However, some children seem better able to control their antisocial tendencies when tight external controls are present. Obviously, the specifics of each program's approach and its prior success with various types of youngsters needs to be explored before enrollment.

Much the same issues exist with other private boarding schools, except that these programs seem to vary greatly in degree of structure and in how they deal with individual differences. Programs that welcome individual differences exist, as do programs that exclude students with special problems. Sourcebooks describing boarding and military schools are available in most bookstores. Consulting several different facilities would appear to be important before a decision is made.

HOME SCHOOLING

Rarely, parents give up all hope of finding an acceptable placement for their child. Often in desperation, they turn to home schooling. Exercising their options under laws that exist in many states, parents keep their child at home, purchase text and school materials, and follow a prescribed curriculum. Local associations of parents frequently exist to offer support and guidance.

For parents who feel that they understand and manage their child as no one else can, this seems like a plausible option. Certainly individual attention can be provided, and the potential parent–school friction can be eliminated in instances where behavior or learning problems accompany ADHD.

The downside to home schooling, however, warrants careful consideration, too. Parents who take on the demanding job of teacher on top of the demanding job of parent may find they end up doing neither well. This is especially true if your child is extremely symptomatic for ADHD, has accompanying conduct or oppositional problems, or has difficulty learning. To teach a difficult child all day and then slip into the afterschool role of a parent who must both discipline and nurture is extremely demanding.

There are other considerations, too. The child with learning problems may require the most experienced and skilled of teachers. In some instances, parents may simply lack the skills to teach their child. Peer relationships is another issue. Already at risk for social skills deficiencies, the child with ADHD who is home schooled is further deprived of a chance to develop these skills. He or she may become quite isolated from peers and may risk long-term social problems. A child who is taught at home may find himself or herself increasingly unaware of the rules for social exchange, or of the topics and interests that are common to peers, and may lack acquaintances with whom to interact. Special effort must be made, therefore, to ensure that the home-schooled child is provided meaningful opportunities for social interaction.

THE BEST OPTION FOR YOUR CHILD

Although potentially bewildering to parents, the diversity of educational programs available in many communities across the United States is quite advantageous to the child with ADHD. This is so because children with ADHD are themselves so varied. Selecting the best option requires a careful evaluation of the child as well as knowledge regarding educational resources and special program eligibility. You are encouraged to seek out the most knowledgeable and qualified professionals to assist you in this task. Of course, the better informed you are about available options and resources, the better you can be in advocating for your child.

Chapter 12

Classroom Techniques

The preceding two chapters addressed how to qualify your child with ADHD for special services and where to educate your child. This chapter explores techniques that can be used in the classroom to best educate the child with ADHD.

Before discussing specifics of instruction, some perspective is in order. No parent can expect to call the shots within his or her child's classroom. That prerogative is the teacher's. Parents who attempt to tell a classroom teacher how to do his or her job will probably alienate their most important ally, their child's classroom teacher. Yet we have seen that outside input, sometimes directly from a parent, may be required. This chapter contains ideas to assist you in your role as your child's advocate. It is cautioned, however, that development of a cooperative, open relationship with your child's teacher, as well as a certain amount of diplomacy, may be required before these ideas can be conveyed to him or her. We also caution that no amount of parental advocacy can substitute for the expert instruction of a quality teacher. No plan yet devised is half so valuable as a good teacher.

GOAL OF EDUCATION

At its core, education's goal is to teach academic skills—that is, initially to teach basic skills in reading, spelling, and mathematics, and later more advanced subjects like science and social studies. With their hands full attempting to meet this daunting task, teachers cannot be expected simultaneously to "cure" ADHD. Even if that is their intent, no educational method for doing so exists. Thus, more modest educational goals must be selected.

Just as the goal at home is to lessen the impact of ADHD and to encourage development of good habits, much the same is true at school. An ideal program for a student with ADHD is one that prevents his or her attentional or self-control problems from hindering learning. That is, as is true for students in general, the student with ADHD should be viewed as benefiting most from school when he or she is able to acquire academic competencies. By understanding the nature of ADHD, educators can make modifications to help ensure that learning does occur and that academic competencies do develop.

EDUCATIONAL TECHNIQUES

Securing Attention before Directions

The first step in instruction is following directions, and the first step in following directions is attending to them. Yet, students with ADHD are apt to miss verbal directions because they are physically occupied with something else or their mind wanders. The child who is absorbed in rolling a pencil repetitively off the desk or is daydreaming about afterschool baseball games will miss directions. Work productivity will suffer and skill development will lag.

Thus, good teachers have learned the crucial first step of securing attention when working with students with ADHD. Many teachers request the class's attention, then pause until all eyes are upon them. More than other students, the child with ADHD, of course, may require special treatment. He or she may then require direct eye contact with the teacher before instructions are provided. *For some children with ADHD, eye contact with the teacher may be required virtually continuously throughout the presentation of directions. Generally, teachers have found that eye contact is the best guarantee of focused attention.*

Checking To Ensure Understanding

Students are even more likely to attend to verbal directions if the instructions are followed by an immediate check for understanding. A teacher's individual verification that the message was understood furnishes the student with a motive for paying attention (so as to look good and avoid embarrassment). The quick check also guarantees that key points are understood or that directions can be followed. Some teachers require students with ADHD to repeat directions, write the essential points out on paper, or highlight essential elements with a pen or pencil if directions are provided in writing.

Preferential Seating

Students seated close to the teacher have a better chance of eye contact during the vital directions phase. This helps them attend and follow directions. They also work better under close teacher scrutiny. *Off-task behavior is most easily noticed and redirected if the teacher is close at hand and has a direct line of vision* to the student. *Likewise, it is often easier for the teach-er to notice and encourage on-task, productive behav-ior when the child is close by.*

Reducing Classroom Distractions

Placement of a child with ADHD close to distractions such as a pencil sharpener, a window, or noisy class-mates is unwise. The commonsense notion that novel stimuli or excessive noise distract children with ADHD seems to be true. If your child's teacher has not already considered reducing classroom distractions, it may be a good idea to raise the idea. The best location must, however, be left to the teacher's discretion.

More radical attempts to control stimulation are generally not suggested. For instance, it was once advo-cated that classrooms be stripped of all potential dis-tracting stimuli (e.g., colorful bulletin boards, win-dows, noisy tile flooring). It was hoped that by lowering the general distraction level, this "stimulus reduction" technique would aid children with ADHD. It was also suggested that some children be placed in three-sided study carrels or facing barren walls. However, these procedures have failed to be supported by empirical research.

Shortening Assignments/Providing Breaks

Children with ADHD can often complete short assign-ments but not long ones. Shortening assignments can help them. As an example, the child who tires, drifts off-task, or quits a 20-minute spelling assignment may do adequately on a 10-minute assignment. Such a re-duction is particularly wise if the child can actually master the skill with a briefer assignment.

In addition, repetitious work, such as arithmetic computations or copying from a dictionary, requires careful scrutiny. Since deficits underlying ADHD may include lack of sustained effort when reward levels are low, presenting low-interest, low-stimulation tasks to a child with ADHD risks exaggerating his or her deficits. Tasks of this type not only reduce attention to task but they invite behavior problems and contribute to long-term discouragement. For many children, repeated practice is not necessary to master a skill. For students with ADHD, it makes sense to determine if the assigned exercises are really necessary. *Reducing assignment lengths or inserting breaks may be especially important when tedious and uninteresting work must be completed.*

Making Assignments
More Interesting and Stimulating

Like children without ADHD, many children with ADHD benefit from novel presentations and more stimulating subject matter instead of repetitive or tedious drills. For example, inserting colored type into the midst of a lengthy passage may help recapture a child's flagging attention. Switching type fonts, altering shapes of objects to be counted, providing texture (e.g., sandpaper letters) or allowing the use of new or different writing tools midway through long assignments may help. These considerations seem to matter most on simple, rote tasks.

Of course, identifying the child's unique interests and skills so that they can be capitalized upon may help, especially on more complex tasks. For instance, a seventh-grade boy who quickly tires of percentage problems may work far longer if computing batting averages of a favorite baseball player (also a percentage problem). Or the child who shows minimal interest in a generic writing assignment may light up at the prospect of writing about a favorite subject such as space travel.

Capitalizing on Strengths, Avoiding Weakness

By the same token, *identifying and using a child's strengths to help him or her succeed, while at the same time avoiding the child's weaknesses, may aid motivation and attention.* For instance, a child with ADHD who is plagued by fine motor problems but blessed with language strengths may require teaching modifications. Failure to reduce written assignments for this child guarantees failure. However, allowing the child to report his or her understanding of class material orally, as opposed to in writing, can help enormously. These modifications are likely not only to make this child successful but may enhance his or her self-image. As pointed out in Chapter 6, a psychoeducational evaluation may help pinpoint individual strengths and weaknesses, thus permitting intelligent educational planning.

CLASSROOM PROGRAMS FOR IMPROVING BEHAVIOR AND INCREASING PRODUCTIVITY

Positive Attention and Rewards

For the child who finds too few rewards inherent in completing work (i.e., the bored, disinterested student), external rewards can be added. The simplest and potentially most plentiful rewards are teacher praise and attention. When appropriate behavior (e.g., sitting with attention focused and working) is followed by attention and praise, this behavior may be strengthened. Teachers, owing mostly to their heavy work demands, often fail to notice and praise appropriate behavior promptly and frequently enough to produce much positive impact. To counteract this shortcoming, *programs that encourage monitoring of a particular student's behavior and praising him or her, if warranted, are often suggested for children with ADHD.* Some of the suggested plans are simple, yet clever. For example, Russell Barkley and his colleagues have suggested placing a large smiling face adjacent to the classroom clock so that each time the teacher glances at the clock he or she is reminded to check on the identified student. If on-task, the child would be praised, if off-task, the child would be ignored or reprimanded. The smiling face reminder may help assure 15–20 daily chances for praise. Of course, timers with chimes or other devices can work just as well as reminders.

Incentive Programs and Token Economies

As valuable as are attention and praise, they often lack sufficient potency to promote ongoing motivation. Added incentives are frequently required. *It is known that the addition of rewards can increase work productivity and improve behavior. These incentives might be special privileges, such as added recess time or serving as line leader, or tangible rewards, such as baseball cards or stickers.* The tangible rewards are often referred to as "backup reinforcers."

In the simplest form, incentives may be dispensed for successful performance, without a detailed, prearranged or formal plan. A teacher might merely state, "If you complete all your worksheets this morning, then you can be line leader for recess." The teacher should build flexibility into these plans by considering work demands, the student's current behavior, and available rewards.

A token economy, a prearranged system of assigning points for acceptable behavior and trading those points for rewards, expands and formalizes this idea of positive consequences for successful behavior. Either academic performance or conduct can be targeted. Consider the program for a student who fails to complete work, as outlined in Figure 12.1. Points may be awarded simply for work completed or, alternatively, for work completed accurately. Thus, one point might be credited for each 10 mathematics problems finished, one point for a spelling worksheet, and two points for answering reading questions. The child's teacher would monitor work production closely and promptly assign points. Points could be exchanged at prescribed times, perhaps at 10:00 A.M., noon, and 2:30 P.M. A unique menu of rewards could be created for each child, or a common menu could be used for several students, or even an entire classroom.

Behavior problems may be treated too. Consider the child who, impulsively and unsolicited, answers classroom questions. This child might be awarded points if he remains quiet for specified time intervals. One point might be awarded for each half-hour of control. Alternatively, the child might be awarded points for performing a behavior incompatible with shouting out answers. Under this plan, the child would be awarded three points each time he raised his hand, waited, and was finally selected by his teacher to answer. Other procedures are discussed later in this chapter for reducing this type of unacceptable behavior.

Chapter 8 in this book emphasized the need for structure when planning interventions for the child

Name:___Sam_____

Date:___7-17-92_____

	Math	Spelling	Reading
1 pt. ▪	10 problems	1 worksheet	1 reading question
Points earned	X̶ X̶ X̶ 4 ③	X̶ 2 3 4 ①	X̶ X̶ 3 4 ②

This sheet is for the time interval between ___8:00____ and __10:00_____. Record points in bank, file this sheet, and begin new sheet at second time listed.

Figure 12.1. Token economy program, used as an incentive to the child to complete work. One point is earned for each 10 math problems, each spelling work sheet, and each reading question completed.

with ADHD. Simply put, structure in this case means that clearly stated expectations exist, and that positive and negative consequences can be quickly dispensed based on behavior. By their very nature, token economies guarantee structure. As an example, a basic set of classroom rules may be posted. These might include: 1) keep hands and feet to self, 2) use inside voice, 3) remain in seat, 4) work on assigned material, 5) raise hand to speak. For each time interval (perhaps 15 minutes) during which these rules were followed, students would be awarded points. Failure in any category, such as leaving one's seat, would result in withholding of points during that interval. Because expectations are clearly outlined, the teacher could supplement points. For example, verbal rewards could be used: "Dan, I liked the way you raised your hand. Why don't you tell the class what your answer is." Little attention is required to correct inappropriate behaviors, and reprimands and redirections can occur clearly and easily: "Betsy, remember to follow rule number 2." This direction could be used to tell a student to modulate her voice tone without dwelling on the specifics of her misbehavior or giving her undue teacher attention.

Although token economies may appear simple, they can be complex. Selecting an appropriate reward menu, revising it periodically as interest for some items or privileges wanes, properly calibrating the price of menu items, providing sufficiently prompt and numerous trade-in times, and selecting reasonable target behaviors with fair point values are among the demands of an effective program. When an incentive or token program fails, or when initial success ceases (both of which are common), a careful revision of the plan can often put things back on track. Expert advice, such as from a special education teacher trained in behavior modification, a counselor, or a psychologist, may be required.

To recap, token economies offer several advantages in working with the child with ADHD:

1. They can be targeted to either academic performance or classroom behavior.
2. By their nature, they guarantee structure.
3. They can be modified and revised to fit the changing needs, interests, or circumstances of the student.

Reprimands and Redirection

Most teachers and parents would prefer to rely on positive consequences. In an ideal world, praise and love would overcome all problems. Empirical research, however, has shown that *reprimands and redirection (verbally instructing the child back to a task or indicating acceptable behavior to them) promote on-task behavior, productivity, and suitable classroom behavior.* For many children, reprimands may actually be essential for school success. Thus, it would be wrong to expect your child's teacher to forgo reprimands or to use a program consisting only of positive attention and praise. Of course, some reprimands are better than others. Repeated or severe reprimands can demoralize students and damage their self-esteem. "Prudent" reprimands, those that are delivered in a calm, firm, consistent, and immediate manner, are advocated over those that are overly emotional, vague, or delayed. Besides greater effectiveness in promoting desired behaviors, reprimands of this type are less likely to damage self-esteem and hamper motivation to succeed.

Response Cost

Response cost is a penalty technique involving loss of privileges, rewards, or tokens based on the occurrence of unacceptable behavior. Response cost can be used as an aspect of a token economy program (previously discussed) or as a separate procedure, such as when an expected privilege is revoked because of misbehavior. *Often children with ADHD require immediate negative consequences to deter inappropriate behavior or to help stop it once it has occurred.* Thus, penalty techniques such as response cost and time-out (discussed next) may be vital. These techniques can help the student with ADHD inhibit inappropriate responding, such as shouting out or hitting.

It is easy to incorporate response cost into a token economy. Points may be accumulated for work productivity and acceptable behavior but lost whenever unacceptable behavior occurs, such as hitting a peer or leaving one's seat. To promote fairness and avoid arbitrary penalties, unacceptable behavior and its penalty value are often spelled out in advance.

A variant of the traditional response cost technique incorporating electronic sophistication has been devised by Michael Gordon, a psychologist at the State University of New York at Syracuse. Called the Attention Trainer, Gordon's device is a small plastic apparatus that sits on the student's desk and credits a point once each minute, presuming that the student is on task, working, and following class rules. The student can easily glance at the device's face to determine his or her point total. Importantly, the teacher is equipped with a portable transmitter capable of subtracting from the child's total from a distance. Points would be subtracted for rule violations, just as they would when other response costs procedures are used. The Attention Trainer's precision, its portability, and the convenience of point tabulation have made it popular in trials with teachers. Research studies have shown it to be effective as well.

Response costs can also be used without a formal token economy. This is especially helpful for the child with ADHD who remains in a regular classroom. As an example, a particularly loud and disruptive student might be given a deck of coupons at the start of each school day. Each coupon might signify a privilege, such as recess, free time to interact with a classmate, access to a preferred location in the classroom, and so on. The student would retain each coupon and would exchange it for the indicated privilege unless a rule violation occurred. Each violation would result in the teacher confiscating one coupon. The fact that penalties follow immediately upon the occurrence of misbehavior and the conspicuousness of the loss (the student sees the confiscation) often makes response cost effective for students with ADHD.

Time-Out

Chapter 8 discussed time-out as a control strategy for home use. As indicated there, *time-out can be an especially successful strategy for children with ADHD, but only under certain circumstances. Unfortunately, those circumstances, which include a pleasing environment from which the child can be excluded so that a negative consequence is experienced, are rarer at school than at home.* At home, most children find it unpleasant to be sent out of the family room or away from the family's center of action. Being isolated from the interactions and activities of the family is unpleasant. However, many students enjoy being sent from their classroom to an isolation area. Rather than a negative consequence, isolation may thus actually be experienced as a reward! Practical problems exist as well. An isolation area may not be available, and many children with ADHD refuse to go willingly. In addition, the classroom may be disrupted if time-out is used under the wrong circumstances, since some children may struggle or have a tantrum, especially when the procedure is first used.

Still, there are times when traditional time-out can be used. A special classroom setting may include its own isolation room to be used for time-out. However, an isolated area, a less-restrictive option than an isolation room, can often be adapted to a special class setting as well. If the teacher makes class instruction interesting enough, and particularly if attention is plentiful or rewards are possible (e.g., a token economy), time-out can work well.

Variations on traditional time-out may be easier to implement. For example, a teacher may set up a classroom so that students can be awarded points on an ongoing basis, perhaps every 10 minutes. With frequent rewards possible, misbehavior can be dealt with by a nonexclusionary time-out. A misbehaving student may have his point card turned down, denoting that he or she is briefly ineligible to receive rewards. After a short interval during which rewards are withheld, the card could be turned up, denoting renewed eligibility for rewards. Another alternative to exclusionary time-out involves a clock whose accumulated time is exchangeable for points and rewards. The clock is simply stopped for brief intervals when a specified misbehavior occurs. Besides ease of implementation, these nonexclusionary time-out procedures may be less damaging to self-esteem and less demoralizing than the exclusionary options. Teachers who understand the time-out principle can devise similar programs.

Home–School Incentive Programs

Sometimes parents must assist classroom teachers with a home–school incentive program to help their children become productive and learn to control their behavior. Although the interval between behavior at school and consequences at home is necessarily long (sometimes 8 or 10 hours), home–school incentive plans can nonetheless be powerful. Happily, a reward of video games upon arrival home, or a chance to do a favorite activity with parents, may motivate work completion and good behavior in ways that a school program cannot. Figure 12.2 is an example of a "daily report card" that is used to convey school performance to parents. A reward menu at home could also be included. Most often, parents sign the form each day so their child can transport it back to the teacher.

Daily Report Card

Name: Ken

Date: 10-17-92

Following school rules

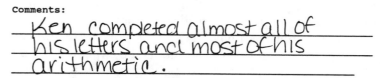

Getting work done

Good Job   Okay   Try Harder Next Time

Comments: Ken completed almost all of his letters and most of his arithmetic.

Figure 12.2. Daily report card to motivate the child and inform parents of child's performance.

Besides providing motivation, home–school programs keep parents informed. They may also help promote a closer parent–teacher alliance. Shortcomings in the student's educational program sometimes are exposed by this type of program. It is easy to see that things are going poorly at school if each day's report indicates unacceptable behavior and/or poor work completion. Obviously, changes can be made more easily when parents and teachers work together closely. Even schools that are reluctant to provide special services or modify classroom assignments may consent to using home–school incentive plans. For some students with ADHD, a home–school program may be the only adjustments the school will endorse.

School Suspension

You may be one of the unfortunate parents threatened with suspension of your child. The logic here is self-evident. The child who violates rules too often or too grievously is sent home as a punishment. Beyond the intent of penalizing the child, the procedure may be designed to heighten parents' awareness and enlist their cooperation. An unspoken assumption seems to be that if the parents are involved, pressure to behave will be exerted on the student.

Although effective for some students, suspensions fail for many children with ADHD. This is because many such children have already been penalized so frequently that a single big penalty has little impact. After all, how can one consequence be expected to curtail a variety of potential bad behaviors over the course of an entire school day? Even big penalties like suspensions may be futile because of the notorious inability of children with ADHD to anticipate consequence. Moreover, there are concerns that this type of exclusion may violate the rights of students with disabilities. If school personnel suggest suspension, it is generally wise to try a more thoughtful program involving rewards and response cost or time-out before reverting to the more drastic option.

REVISING EXPECTATIONS
TO INCREASE MOTIVATION

Judicious Assignment of Grades

Grades are assigned to inform parents and to motivate students. For the child with ADHD, these purposes may need to be reviewed carefully and grades correspondingly adjusted.

If your child is affected with ADHD of sufficient magnitude to cause school problems, then you need frequent communication with his or her classroom teacher. Daily or weekly reports about level of performance, work productivity and effort, and conduct/deportment are probably required. Since you are already informed about your child's status, you should expect to find little new from a report card. A report card designed for a student without school problems may be valueless to you. Thus, there is no pressing need for teachers to use low grades to tell you that your child is having trouble. You already know it.

High grades can motivate achieving students to keep up the good work or spur them toward even greater performance. Low grades can motivate a few students to do better. Unfortunately, too often, students with ADHD receive a report card filled with low grades and indications of "needs improvement" in areas such as effort, cooperation, or rule following. For this student, low grades probably do little good. On the contrary, they can do considerable harm to self-esteem and can further erode the student's already-depleted base of motivation. The second purpose of report card grades, to motivate, is thus also hard to accomplish for the student with ADHD.

Consequently, teachers should be encouraged to view the grading system flexibly. Each student's unique circumstances and capabilities need to be considered when marks are assigned. Even when grade values are not altered to reflect unique circumstances, teachers and parents may do well to emphasize daily performance—for example, points earned or work completed—rather than dwelling on semester report card marks. A report card filled with low marks should generally be avoided.

Expectations for Homework

Homework represents a special pitfall for children with ADHD. Put yourself in your child's position by imagining that you are assigned to do a job at your place of employment that is very difficult for you to do. Try as you may, you can seldom finish the assigned tasks, despite putting in a full work day. Your boss is frequently on your case. Now, because you have failed to complete your assigned tasks by day's end, you are told you must take your work home to complete it there. How might you feel about your "homework" assignment? Recall, too, that you are an adult, with all the perspective and understanding that only maturity can bring; assume that you possess adult self-control. Most adults, if they are honest with themselves, would approach their homework with little enthusiasm.

With this perspective in mind, *you should encourage your child's teacher to keep homework assignments within reasonable bounds.* For some students, setting time limits help. For example, parents of elementary school children with ADHD may confine each evening's worktime to 30 minutes, high school students to 60 minutes. If children are unable to complete the necessary material within these limits, then the length of assignments, their composition, or the student's work productivity in class probably should be checked. Only when all other attempts to improve in-class productivity have been tried and have failed, should more homework time be added.

Sometimes overdependence on homework develops. Understandably this can happen because parents can provide the individual attention and direction lacking in a large classroom. Finding that it is easier to slough off the work at school because help awaits them at home, the student may get little done at school. Eventually, the student may complete less and less in class. Parents and teacher must step in if this occurs, often by limiting the amount of work completed at home. The interventions discussed earlier in this chapter probably are needed at these times as well.

Of course, all the advice that parents hear about homework in general also applies to homework and the student with ADHD. Selecting a quiet environment, a consistent time, and providing parental encouragement may well boost work completion. Arranging privileges as rewards to be dispensed immediately after the work is completed may help as well. Of course, just as absolute dos and don'ts about homework make no sense for children without ADHD, absolutes have no role for children with ADHD either. Each child is an individual, and individual judgment and flexibility are required.

ENSURING CLASSROOM SUPPORT

Selecting an Effective Elementary Teacher

The patient, encouraging teacher, filled with energy and willing to accommodate individual needs, is generally the best choice for your child. Sometimes, a regular education teacher who possesses these qualities, plus coincident training in special education, is available. Such an individual should be carefully considered. If your child is in a special education setting, teachers with training in either behavior management or in behavior problems, or both, may be preferred. You may want to ask about the teacher's experience with children with ADHD. Of course, your choice of teacher in the public schools is probably limited, or even non-existent. *Nonetheless, the quality of teaching is so important that you are encouraged to explore the possibilities of selecting a teacher.* Alternatives to public school were discussed in the preceding chapter. Occasionally, going outside of public education to secure an exceptional teacher is justified.

Extra Guidance During Transition to Junior High School

For many children, the transition to junior high school is especially difficult. The introduction to departmentalized instruction (i.e., one instructor for English, another for mathematics) presents the severest challenge. Each teacher may expect something slightly different in terms of work completion, in-class behavior, and homework. Besides this, teachers may not communicate with each other. As a result, homework demands may vary wildly, with some evenings free of assignments and other evenings with heavy demands. Organization, such as keeping track of assignments and work materials, and budgeting of time become paramount. Unfortunately, the child with ADHD is apt to be particularly wanting in these skills.

The antidote to the inconsistency of expectations and variable work demands that begin during junior high school (or occasionally earlier) is to find someone capable of adding organization, consistency, and structure to your child's day. Usually, this person is located at the school (as opposed to a parent or a private tutor), and often is a school staff member with primary instructional responsibility. For example, a resource teacher may be a liaison to each of the classroom teachers, thereby ensuring that the student is recording work to be completed, consistently taking textbooks home, returning completed assignments, preparing for tests, and generally keeping his or her "academic head above water." In some settings, guidance counselors have established methods and procedures to help accomplish these tasks. Among the devices are forms for recording assignments and weekly feedback to parents, and guidelines for homework completion. Even for the child who has succeeded in elementary school, this type of support may be necessary. *If your child has been identified as having ADHD, you are encouraged to monitor his or her progress closely during the transition from self-contained elementary instruction to departmentalized junior high instruction.*

SUMMARY

In summary, the following techniques have been suggested for use with some children with ADHD:

1. To help the child attend to and follow directions, the teacher should establish and maintain eye contact with the child while giving directions.
2. Once directions have been given, the teacher should check with the child to ensure that directions have been understood.
3. Noise and other stimuli can distract the child with ADHD; avoid seating the child near classroom distractions.
4. Reduce assignment lengths or insert breaks when repetitious or tedious work must be completed, es-

pecially if the child can master the skill with a briefer assignment.

5. Concentrate on novel presentations and stimulating subject matter as much as possible.

6. Identifying and using a child's strengths, while avoiding his or her weaknesses, can aid motivation.

7. Use programs to monitor a student's behavior, incorporating praise as warranted. Other rewards and incentives are also frequently important for increasing work productivity and improving behavior.

8. Verbal reprimands and redirection can be used to promote on-task behavior, productivity, and suitable classroom behavior. Avoid severe reprimands.

9. Develop a penalty technique involving loss of privileges, rewards, or tokens based on the occurrence of unacceptable behavior, if warranted.

10. Time-out can be an especially effective strategy for children with ADHD but may not work in a classroom setting. Modifications of traditional time-out by withholding eligibility for rewards (e.g., a token economy) may be required.

11. A home–school incentive program based on a "daily report card" may enable parents to assist classroom teachers in helping children become more productive and learn to control their behavior.

12. Although effective for some students, suspensions fail to influence many children with ADHD.

13. To help increase motivation, teachers should be encouraged to view the grading system flexibly and consider each student's unique circumstances and capabilities.

14. Parents should work with teachers to keep homework assignments within reasonable bounds and work to improve in-class productivity.

15. Explore the possibility of selecting teachers with training in behavior management or behavior problems.

16. Monitor the progress of your child during transition from self-contained elementary instruction to departmentalized junior high instruction and, if necessary, find someone capable of adding organization, consistency, and structure to your child's day.

CONCLUSION

You may best champion your child's educational cause if you are aware of some of the special classroom techniques that children with ADHD often require. This chapter enumerates some of those techniques. However, developing a working alliance with your child's teacher(s) is essential if any of the plans herein discussed are to receive their fullest and most effective implementation.

Chapter 13

Counseling, Biofeedback, and Other Interventional Approaches

Specially designed school services, behavior management at home, and medication are the most typically used and most widely accepted interventions for ADHD. However, other approaches exist as well. This chapter contains information about these other techniques.

PROFESSIONAL COUNSELING AND PSYCHOTHERAPY

Individual Therapy

It is unreasonable to expect that a series of sessions of psychotherapy (i.e., a psychologist or therapist meeting alone with a child in an office) can "cure" all of your child's ADHD symptoms. As discussed in Chapter 2, the symptoms of ADHD are caused by malfunctions in the central nervous system. They are not caused by internal conflicts, misdirected motives, lack of self-worth, or the similar issues that individual therapy addresses.

Simply because individual therapy may fail to "cure" ADHD does not mean that it is valueless, however. Children and teens with ADHD experience the same self-doubts, conflicts, worries, and confusion as anyone else. In fact, they probably experience these more frequently and harshly than their peers because of their history of failure and because they sense their lack of self-control. Just as individual therapy helps children and teenagers without ADHD when these problems occur, it can also help those with ADHD. When a caring, supportive or understanding person is called for, an individual therapist may be in order. By training and temperament, therapists may offer help unavailable elsewhere.

Individual therapy may aid specific problems, too. A teenager frustrated by recurring peer rejection may gain perspective and learn alternative strategies for dealing with peers through therapy. So, too, can a child whose repeated misbehavior has led to feelings of rejection from parents and siblings. Even though therapy is incapable of preventing the misbehavior, it may deter further damage to self-esteem if the child understands the causes of the misbehavior and can put others' responses to him or her in their proper light.

Family Therapy

Not surprisingly, family friction often results from the stresses of living with a child with ADHD. Parents may accuse each other of mishandling their child's behavior or of actually promoting problem behavior. They may differ about how to handle discipline. Conflicts about roles may arise. One or both parents may develop an overly close or overly distant relationship with the affected child.

Siblings are likely to be affected too. Sometimes, deeply held feelings of resentment are present among brothers and sisters whose needs have been overlooked in the family's effort to help the most difficult child. Occasionally, these children themselves begin to misbehave as a way to seek attention. This is especially likely when the more-difficult-to-manage sibling begins to improve through treatment. A therapeutic approach that works with the entire family may be beneficial at these times.

Cognitive Behavior Therapy

Like the behavioral training for parents discussed in Chapter 8, cognitive behavior therapy can be provided by an individual therapist (sometimes in group settings, too). Often a psychologist provides the services. Although behavior modification principles are used in both approaches, there are important differences. Cognitive behavior therapy works directly with the child or teenager, rather than with a parent or teacher. The approach attempts to train the child to exercise better self-control or to respond reflectively as opposed to impulsively.

Activities involve changing the *cognitions* (thinking) that underlie unacceptable *behavior*—hence the term *cognitive/behavioral*. For example, children may be taught the skill of self-monitoring by being provided feedback about their behavior and then by learning to rate their own behavior accurately. Over time in such a program, rewards are dispensed based on how accurately the child learns to evaluate his or her own behavior. The notion is that children with ADHD fail to monitor their own behavior closely enough, and when this happens, they are apt to behave in a poorly controlled fashion. If, so the reasoning goes, they were taught to self-appraise and self-monitor better, they would behave better. Thus, impulsive, poorly planned behavior may give way to more reflective and better-planned behavior.

Children usually participate in a series of training or therapy sessions, perhaps 10–20. The programs are often sequential and may be quite detailed. Training usually moves from simple to complex skills. Some programs teach detailed problem-solving skills in which children are taught to identify problems, plan a strategy, define a solution, and then rate themselves on how effectively the solution worked. As training proceeds, children are taught the necessary steps to solve problems. Early in training the therapist may guide the child through problem solving with verbal directions. Later the child is encouraged to guide his or her own behavior with verbal directions spoken aloud. Still later, internal or "cognitive" directions are to be employed by the child to lead himself or herself to acceptable actions. Throughout training, behavioral principles, such as rewarding mastery of the training steps, are used by the therapist.

Some children appear to learn to slow themselves and exercise better problem-solving skills using this approach. Yet, proof of the technique's effectiveness is generally lacking. Even when successful training occurs, questions remain about whether the child retains these skills after training stops (i.e., in the months and years to come) or generalizes them in other settings (i.e., on the playground or with friends rather than just in the therapist's office). Skills would appear to be retained and generalized best when parents and teachers are aware of training and are capable of rewarding children when real-world applications are made. Although cognitive behavior therapy is a potential adjunct to traditional treatment such as medication and parent training, it cannot be regarded as a principal treatment for ADHD. Again, there is no evidence that it can "cure" ADHD.

Group Therapy To Teach Social Skills

Many children with ADHD have problems getting along with others their age. It is hardly surprising that the high activity, talkativeness, social intrusiveness, and poor frustration tolerance that characterize many children with ADHD would alienate peers. Despite good intentions, many children with ADHD find that they have few consistently functioning friendships. It is unfortunate that, due to impulse and judgment deficits, a child with ADHD is likely to be without enduring friendships.

Treatment may help, but many affected children remain isolated even after being properly treated with medicine, with special school services, or with behavior management at home. Most of these children are not incapable of learning to get along better; they simply find these skills hard to learn. Often a direct teaching approach, such as social skills teaching, helps.

Using the social skills teaching approach, groups of same-age and same-sex children can function as a laboratory to teach social skills that most children learn naturally, that is, without any particular help. Trained therapists or psychologists can move children through a training curriculum that teaches, step-by-step, how to get along. Unacceptable behaviors can be isolated and reduced by direct feedback. For instance, bragging, bossing, belittling peers, dominating conversations, and the like can be addressed directly in the group setting. Candid feedback and negative consequences (e.g., response cost as discussed in Chapter 8) can be dispensed by impartial professionals with an effectiveness unattainable by family members. Feedback from peers themselves can also help. More important, skills essential for acquiring and maintaining friends can be encouraged in a group setting by using rewards, modeling, role-playing, and practice over a period of weeks. Among the important skills that can be addressed in this fashion are how to initiate a conversation, ways to sustain a conversation without dominating, how to select a suitable topic, complimenting peers, taking turns, giving and accepting feedback, and handling teasing and disappointment.

Most social skill development programs are practical and no-nonsense. Group members work together with therapists to develop a list of "dos and don'ts." These are tried in contrived role-playing situations within the group, and then are tried outside the group. To maximize effectiveness, parents and teachers should be informed of the particular skills being developed, and are encouraged to reward or prompt skill usage outside the group. Homework assignments and monitoring of skill usage in the real world may be part of the program, too.

Most social skill groups meet for a minimum of 10–15 sessions, usually weekly. Since these skills are expected to develop by relatively slow increments, many children participate in such groups on an ongoing basis. Others are exposed to the basic curriculum only. For the former youngsters, the group may not only help them develop new skills, it may also offer support, a chance for acceptance, and fraternity. In the multidisciplinary practice at Phoenix [Arizona] Children's Hospital, social skill groups provide an added advantage in that the therapist is allowed to observe, first hand, medication's effectiveness. Precise reports of the child's behavior can then be made to the prescribing physician, should any of the group members be receiving medication for ADHD.

BIOFEEDBACK

Biofeedback refers to a variety of techniques used to teach individuals to control their bodies through the use of feedback. For example, headache patients with extreme tension in the frontalis muscles of the forehead often benefit by learning to relax those muscles. A laboratory apparatus that measures changes in tension can be integrated with a feedback mechanism, such as a light or tone, so that muscle-tension changes in the desired direction can be signaled to the patient. Over time, patients can learn to relax their muscles in progressive degrees.

As mentioned early in this book, some researchers (e.g., Joel Lubar and colleagues at the University of Tennessee in Knoxville) have speculated that ADHD is associated with underarousal in the brain. Although motorically overactive, individuals with ADHD may lack sufficient nervous system arousal to attend well or to control impulses. Citing studies accumulated over a period of more than 15 years, Lubar and colleagues have presented information suggesting that the underarousal suspected in individuals with ADHD is evident on an electroencephalogram (EEG, graphic record produced by an electroencephalograph, which measures the electrical activity of the brain). More important, it is presumed the underarousal actually causes ADHD symptoms. If more normal arousal levels could be accomplished, it is argued, then ADHD symptoms ought to be diminished or eliminated.

This is where some researchers have suggested that biofeedback may play a role. They contend that by using currently available, sophisticated EEG devices, patterns of electrical activity can be altered to produce enhanced arousal. For example, individuals may be connected to an EEG device through leads attached at the scalp so that some aspects of the brain's electrical activity can be measured. The individual looks at a computer screen that provides feedback. As waves reflecting higher levels of arousal appear, the computer screen provides an encouraging signal to the individual, such as a circle that grows in size. Gradually, individuals, including children, reportedly learn to increase the amount of desired brain waves and correspondingly decrease undesirable waves.

Case studies collected over several years, and more recently controlled studies as well, suggest that as EEG changes occur, ADHD symptoms abate. There are also reports of improved academic status, presumably due to the individual's newly acquired capability to arouse attention and sustain concentration.

Although in relatively narrow use at the time of this writing, EEG biofeedback to treat ADHD is being promoted as a nonpharmacologic (medicine-free) approach to treating ADHD. Dr. Lubar's writings seem to imply that for some children, a combination of medication and biofeedback may be required, at least at the outset of biofeedback training. It is also noteworthy that the training advocated is quite lengthy: 40–80 sessions spread over several months. The application of this treatment then would require considerable time and funding.

How effective this type of biofeedback will be in the long run in treating ADHD has yet to be proven. The professional community will no doubt be watching for additional empirical studies or for wider distribution of the studies already conducted.

MARTIAL ARTS TRAINING

Martial arts, such as karate, Judo, or Tai Chi have been advocated by some as a means of helping children with ADHD. The rationale here seems to be that children benefit by learning to respond to clear expectations (such as those that occur during training), and that the self-discipline required to complete training may profit children with ADHD. By learning to concentrate their attention, follow directions, and exercise restraint, it is believed by some that children can learn skills that are potentially generalizable outside of training. If this supposition has been borne out by research, that research is not widely known.

If beneficial at all, it is more likely that martial arts training aids the child or teenager with ADHD in other ways. Perhaps participation in an organized training sequence that builds skills may lead to increased self-confidence—particularly for boys, who are apt to ascribe self-worth to physical competence and an ability to "take care of themselves." Other advantages may result from the very act of channeling physical activity or by promoting contact with, and possibly acceptance from, peers with whom training is done.

Although martial arts training may be worthwhile, uncontrolled rough play, such as emulating martial arts heroes in the movies, may be bad. Children with ADHD seem especially prone to act out the roles of heroes (or villains) with martial arts expertise that they have watched in movies or on television. Thus, young boys may insist on demonstrating high kicks or karate chops they have seen in the movies when friends come to visit. This type of behavior is prone to degenerate into fights and hurt feelings. Children with ADHD are likely to overdo such rough play and alienate peers. It is generally wise to discourage quickly this type of behavior and to avoid allowing children with preexisting tendencies toward rough play and underregulation of impulses to watch excessively violent movies or television shows.

MATCHING EXPECTATIONS TO CAPABILITIES

Admittedly, matching expectations to capabilities is a general notion rather than a specific treatment. But the idea is so important to your child's longer-term adjustment and happiness that it merits mention.

This book has stressed repeatedly that children with ADHD have characteristic, constitutional differences that distinguish them from other children, and that these differences are usually longstanding and resistant to easy change. No one knows your child better than you; you have the best vantage point to discern your child's temperament. Study your child. You will know how long and under what circumstances attention can be maintained, what frustrates, what discourages, what precipitates conflict with peers or siblings, and when impulsivity is likely to result in problem behavior. At the same time, you can recognize those instances where success is most probable, and what strengths exist.

This information is essential because it provides a basis for guiding your child toward success and away from failure. Many children with ADHD become demoralized because they repeatedly fail. To the extent that repeated failure can be avoided, your child is likely to feel happier and more successful. Some situations are so destined to produce failure that they should be avoided. Yet, repeatedly well-intentioned parents expect their child with ADHD to attend a church service, sit quietly with absolutely no diversions during a long car ride, exercise self-control in a room filled with rambunctious children (e.g., at a poorly structured outing), or play a frustrating video game without temper outbursts. If these situations are a sure bet for failure, consider avoiding them altogether. If unavoidable, it might help to simplify the task or add structure to the activity (see Chapter 8).

If your child does participate (total avoidance of frustration wouldn't be acceptable anyway), then don't be surprised if failure, discouragement, and anger ensue. Try to avoid your own overreaction to these occurrences. To place a child with ADHD in a difficult situation without revising expectations for focused and well-controlled behavior would be terribly unfair. Learn to match your expectations to your child's capabilities. He or she is not equally capable as siblings or friends in all situations; learn to protect your child from pointless frustration and comedowns.

The flip side of this coin is to recognize your child's talents and find ways that he or she can use them. The failure-plagued child often has a crucial need for success. Thus, parents can help the sports-minded child feel good about his or her ability by signing up the child to play in a local soccer or baseball league. Also in this connection, trips to the ballpark may afford chances for your child to exhibit knowledge about baseball facts. Or a baseball card collection may give your child a sense of pride in being able to marshal substantial amounts of information as well as or better than peers, at least in some situations. Similarly, the child who loves animals and is good with them may benefit from assisting in a veterinarian's office or volunteering at an animal shelter. Activities such as these that do not require intensive focusing of attention enhance success as they promote feelings of self-worth.

PROVIDING A PREDICTABLE HOME ROUTINE

Perhaps the suggestion given most often to parents of children with ADHD is to make their children's schedules predictable. To the extent possible, children with ADHD should arise, eat, complete chores, tackle homework, recreate, and sleep at regular times and places. The reasoning behind this is obvious. The external structure provided by a rote system means that fewer demands are placed on the child's deficient coping skills. Regular expectations, if successfully met, help turn into good habits. This general recommendation makes sense, especially if parents avoid going overboard and resist the temptation to become too rigid. A generally understood routine is probably even more helpful if coupled with frequently imposed parental structure in the form of clear directions and immediate consequences (as discussed in Chapter 8).

AVOIDING OVERDOING HOME TREATMENT

For the minority of parents who tend to overdo their youngsters' treatment, it is important to emphasize that although structure and routine are generally wise, when taken to extremes they can become counterproductive. No child tolerates a schedule in which there is no room for spontaneity. Few children can remain resentment-free in the face of unrelenting parental suggestions to "slow down" and "think over your options and then make a plan." The extremely overcoached child may come to view himself or herself as incapable of independent action, or as peculiar and different from his or her peers. Sometimes the ADHD problem is so highlighted that it becomes parents' central focus—at times even the entire family's central concern. Home ceases to be a home and becomes a 24-hour treatment center.

Children with ADHD are first and foremost children, likely to manifest all the unique interests, talents, hopes, and frustrations of other children. Parents need to strike a balance between concern and assistance on the one hand, and tolerance and perspective on the other. Many parents do this wonderfully. All parents are encouraged to examine their own outlook and, if need be, back off a little and relax.

CONCLUSION

Devising a comprehensive intervention plan for your child is best accomplished by working with a professional who is knowledgeable about ADHD. Aside from considering the most conventional interventions— medication, training in behavior management for parents, and educational modifications—your child's professional can help determine what, if any, additional services may be worthwhile. For some children, individual or family counseling, cognitive behavior therapy, or social skills training may be advisable. Less frequently, martial arts training or biofeedback may be suggested. A professional who knows your child and family can also help establish suitable expectations and determine ways to maximize your child's successes.

Chapter 14

Case Examples in Treatment

The preceding six chapters have outlined a variety of potentially helpful methods for treating children with ADHD. One or several of these suggestions may be applied for any particular youngster. The following case studies may help you appreciate the specifics regarding how children with ADHD can be assisted.

HUGH: ADHD AND SPECIAL SCHOOL SERVICES

Hugh's family met with the school psychologist for the first time when Hugh was 6 years old and already manifesting significant behavior problems. His mother and stepfather were unsure why he was so hard to discipline at home. They were hardly surprised that his behavior was equally troublesome at school, but they remained baffled as to the cause of his problems. They had heard of ADHD, but doubted that Hugh had such a disorder.

Although Hugh was strong-willed and active at home, his behavior was worst at school. Hugh seldom sat for an activity, he laughed wildly at classmates' least provocations, and sometimes stubbornly refused teacher requests. As his first-grade year proceeded and he found himself more frequently in trouble, Hugh's behavior worsened. By the end of October he was often sent to the time-out square (see Chapter 12), yet he frequently refused to go. When prompted by his teacher, he became angry and had to be escorted physically to the principal's office. This sequence occurred twice; then Hugh was suspended from school for 3 days.

Equally troublesome, the relationship between Hugh and his teacher, and that between him and his classmates, suffered. He was shunned on the playground or teased. A common insult one first grader might hurl at another was, "You're acting just like Hugh." His teacher's patience had also worn thin. Although she recognized her anger and its origin ("It's unfair to 25 other students when one takes so much time"), she felt powerless to refrain from snapping at Hugh. She ultimately came to dread his morning arrival.

Some school officials were convinced that Hugh's behavior was entirely willful and purposely defiant. Despite the failure of a simple point system for in-class cooperation (happy face for a good day, frowning face for a bad day with accompanying loss of privileges at home), and the use of suspension for disruption, Hugh's teacher and principal rejected the idea he had an emotional or behavior problem. Although sympathetic, the school psychologist believed that the door for special services through a learning disabilities designation was closed. When she administered screening tests to Hugh, he read, spelled, and computed arithmetic problems about as well as other first graders.

The school psychologist asked for a consultation from a child psychologist in private practice, and also sought guidance from the state department of education. The psychologist quickly noted that Hugh's in-office behavior and history were compatible with ADHD. The diagnosis was soon confirmed by a variety of parent- and teacher-completed rating forms. Although the start of therapy with the psychologist and use of behavior management techniques at home resulted in some improvement, school behavior remained unacceptable. Increasingly frustrated, school officials again threatened Hugh with school suspension unless his defiance and disruption stopped.

At this time, the school psychologist was encouraged to conduct a more detailed evaluation. That evaluation found Hugh to be a bright child and free of any memory, perceptual, or fine motor deficits that would hinder learning. His academic skills were found to be solidly average. Personality testing, interview, and rating forms showed no obvious problems with depression, anxiety, or disturbed thinking. Problems with attention, impulse control, cooperation, and interpersonal relationships were documented, however.

Because of Hugh's inability to sustain attention on assigned tasks and his conduct problems, perhaps resulting from impaired anticipation of consequences, Hugh obviously required altered educational services. As first steps, Hugh's parents and local public school personnel advocated reduction of assignment length, a reward system that provided feedback for success each 5 minutes, and an immediate consequence of time-out in an isolated classroom corner (followed by more stringent isolation if required). To implement this plan, additional personnel in Hugh's classroom (e.g., a teacher's aide), and a staff member to monitor the plan's effectiveness (e.g., a school psychologist, counselor, or special education teacher) would be required. The option of placing Hugh in a self-contained class composed of 10 students, a teacher, and a teacher's aide, and operating on a strict reward system, was held in abeyance in case the less-restrictive approach failed. Unfortunately, school personnel, and most adamantly the school principal, contended that there was no basis for providing Hugh these special services. He was said to be ineligible for special education, and his teacher was said to be unable to check his behavior every 5 minutes or to dispense rewards and punishment without assistance.

The team concluded in an oral summary to his parents that Hugh was not eligible for seriously emotionally disturbed designation either. They argued that his problems resulted from his intentional defiance of authority. A dissenting opinion, offered by the school psychologist, was that although Hugh chose his actions and must be held accountable for them, he nonetheless was operating at a disadvantage compared to his classmates. Among these were severe problems sitting and remaining on task during seatwork and impaired ability to inhibit impulses or weigh consequences. Although it was grudgingly agreed that Hugh indeed had ADHD, and that this disorder was affecting him in school, the team felt they were left with no options for providing him the individualized services he required.

Assistance came from the state department of education, however, when experts from the department encouraged the team to think more broadly regarding Hugh's options. After recognizing that Hugh's behavior was affecting him in school, the school team considered two possible ways to acquire federal services. The first was to designate him as a seriously emotionally disturbed student (see Davila, chap. 10, this volume). The team focused on one emotional characteristic from the federal definition that permits identification if there exists "an inability to build or maintain satisfactory relationships with peers and teachers." The team unanimously agreed that this was true of Hugh. In fact, they concurred that his interpersonal status was deteriorating daily. Clearly, Hugh's ADHD symptoms were having a severe impact on his interpersonal relations. An additional element of the criteria for seriously emotionally handicapped services calls for the emotional problem to "adversely affect educational performance." In Hugh's case there was little doubt that his performance was suffering. In fact, his emotional problem was so significant that he was excluded from class (i.e., sent home or to the principal's office) for extended time periods.

A second option for securing services was to suggest that Hugh's disorder (ADHD) was exerting a significant negative impact on an important aspect of his life (i.e., school learning) and to seek protection under Section 504 of the Rehabilitation Act of 1973 (see Davila, chap. 10, this volume). As such, Hugh's ADHD condition and the associated failure meant that Hugh was being discriminated against when he was excluded from school. The necessary steps to rectify this discrimination were to implement the plan mentioned earlier. To do so, the school either could use an already-available special educational aide or provide an additional aide (nonspecial education) in Hugh's classroom. Because this approach resulted in less-obvious labeling, it was preferred by Hugh's parents and by some school officials.

Ultimately, Hugh was provided services as a seriously emotionally disturbed student. The combination of behavior management and therapy services with the family and the in-class management/reward plan resulted in a drastic reduction of problems. After an initial period of resistance to the sit-out consequence, Hugh began to respond in a more controlled fashion. He came to recognize when he was about to receive a consequence, a recognition that helped deter some of his impulsive behavior. Equally important, the relationship between Hugh and his teacher improved. He was especially responsive to the 5-minute reward program, but he did poorly if the teacher or aide failed to stick closely to the 5-minute time line. With better control, Hugh came to anticipate rewards he was about to receive for completing work and following rules. Once he stopped disrupting class, his classmates were more accepting of him. Eventually, Hugh had a reasonably successful first-grade year.

JAMES: SPECIAL EDUCATION, MEDICATION, AND BEHAVIOR MANAGEMENT

Ten-year-old James had been identified as having learning disabilities when he was in the third grade. Now a fifth grader, he was continuing to struggle in school despite a daily hour of resource tutoring in reading and language arts. James's classroom teacher reported that he failed to complete classwork, was disorganized, and forgetful. His grades were mostly Fs. James also displayed many ADHD symptoms, including short attention span, distractibility, and social intrusiveness; impulsivity seemed to underlie many of his problems.

At the encouragement of his teacher, James was taken to his pediatrician. The pediatrician collected a health and developmental history revealing a healthy child whose developmental rate was slightly delayed linguistically but advanced motorically. James had always been overactive. His exuberance had been noted as early as 8 months. His play had tended to be rough, and he never tolerated sedentary activities. Peers accepted him, although he was often too talkative. An informal teacher report showed symptoms of inattention, impulsivity, and failing work. These were confirmed in a telephone conversation between James's teacher and his pediatrician.

In a meeting with his mother in the pediatrician's office, James was initially well focused. After "warming up," his impulsivity was clear as he investigated items in the examining room while his mother and the physician talked. He was restless, sitting only briefly on the examining table. He asked questions with increasing impertinence, although good-naturedly. The pediatrician noted several facial scrapes, which were due to James's rough, careless, high-energy style of play.

Based on the history and observation, the pediatrician concluded that James was indeed "hyperactive" (ADHD) and was a candidate for treatment with medication. The pediatrician decided to proceed with Ritalin and the family concurred. The initial dosage was 5 milligrams each morning and noon. Possible side effects were explained. The pediatrician inquired and recorded the fact that James had difficulty falling asleep even without medication, a potentially important finding in case sleep problems were noted after the medication was started. James's appetite was good. He had no tics, complaints of headache, or stomachache before medicine was started.

The pediatrician suggested that James start medicine on a Saturday morning. This start, she suggested, allowed two advantages. First, James's parents would be able to observe therapeutic and side effects, should they occur. Second, in the unlikely event that severe side effects should arise, medicine could be stopped quickly. James's parents were encouraged to keep a log of observations—an informal summary of any unusual events, either positive or negative—following the start of medication. She asked that James's parents talk with his teacher by telephone on Wednesday afternoon to identify any changes at school. After the call was completed, parents were to speak with the pediatrician by phone to apprise her of the child's status.

James took his first dose of Ritalin at 8:30 Saturday morning. By 9:30 A.M., his mother noted an important change. James was actually watching television with his younger siblings. There was no fighting or arguing. The parents conferred, but they could not reach a consensus about whether James was sitting stiller. They did both agree that he was getting along better with his brother and sister throughout the morning. James subsequently ate a large midday meal.

A second 5 milligram tablet was administered at 12:30 P.M., and again James's parents noted changes in behavior. From approximately 2:00 P.M. until 4:00 P.M. he watched his father work on a model airplane. Although he left several times, he always returned, sat attentively, and talked in a polite fashion. There were no signs of intrusion, nor did he attempt to dominate the conversation. Soon after 4:00, however, he seemed to be back to his old behavior. He fought with his younger brother, repeatedly taking the younger child's toy, even though his mother had warned him to keep his hands to himself. James ate a large dinner at 6:00 P.M.; there were no complaints about lack of hunger. He went to bed at his normal weekend bedtime of 10:00 without any problems. Improvement in behavior was evident, but was felt by his parents to be less than dramatic overall.

By the time of the parent-to-teacher telephone call on Wednesday, James's teacher had noticed he was completing more work. The teacher volunteered that she had noticed fewer trips to the pencil sharpener. James had remained too talkative, however, and he had had two playground incidents.

When James's mother spoke to the pediatrician, she assured the doctor that James was experiencing no severe side effects from the medicine; however, she also thought the therapeutic effects were inadequate. The pediatrician pointed out that 5 milligrams was a beginning dose, and she suggested an increase to 10 milligrams each morning and at midday, and a 5 milligram dosage at 4:00 P.M. She pointed out that the afternoon dose is often important to ensure that some therapeutic effects exist during crucial social and homework times. The afternoon dose was also designed to lessen any potential rebound effect. This time there was an even more obvious improvement of symptoms, especially at school. James's teacher commented that he now was completing substantially more work and appears to be "better focused." Fewer playground problems had occurred as well. At home, he was "paying better attention and sitting still for quiet activities like he never did before," according to his mother.

Appetite now became a slight problem. James's parents were uncomfortable with his occasional picking at lunch, and they disliked his snacking late in the evening. However, they backed off from demanding he clean his plate, and acquiesced to the high-calorie evening snacks suggested by his pediatrician.

At a 3-month follow-up, James's mother reported that he was making outstanding school progress. Not only was he better able to complete work in class, but his resource teacher reported that he was more attentive and better able to profit from their time together. She commented that the overly fast pace that had previously characterized James's approach to reading had changed. With coaching he now slowed down and sounded out words syllable by syllable. In addition, he seemed to pay better attention to the nature of stories he read aloud for his resource teacher. This allowed him to focus more on comprehension and to use the context of the story to help figure out unknown words.

On the other hand, James's mother told the pediatrician that she was frustrated that his behavior at home was still a problem. Her comments were, "It seems like the Ritalin has solved many of his school problems, but he still talks back too much and there are too many times that he won't cooperate. Maybe I notice these now more that we are less worried about school, but it is a problem." In response to these concerns, the pediatrician suggested the family visit a psychologist knowledgeable about ADHD. The goal was to examine James's home behavior and the ways his parents dealt with his behavior, to determine if alternative discipline methods might help.

The psychologist met only briefly with James during the first office visit. Subsequently, he met with the parents alone; James did not come to this appointment. Each of the first few sessions consisted of the parents outlining their greatest areas of conflict with their son: refusal to follow directions, rough play in the house, and dawdling on chores were three examples. Next, the parents discussed their traditional method of handling the problem: discussion, threats, grounding. Each problem was then reviewed by the psychologist with an attempt to understand behavior in terms of behavior and consequences. Using the steps similar to those outlined in Chapter 8 (see pages 127–133). James's parents and the psychologist together worked out alternative discipline methods. The parents found that using clearer directives helped them tremendously. They also discovered that when they reduced their discussion with James and used the time-out consequence more promptly, James responded much more quickly. Although there was a brief period of resistance and complaints by James, ultimately he became more manageable.

James's parents met with the psychologist for six weekly sessions. To promote independent problem solving, the psychologist asked the parents to describe how they might solve various hypothetical problems. At the conclusion of the sixth session, the parents felt they had mastered the basic ideas of defining problems, targeting behaviors, and promptly applying consequences. They were fast learners. A 1-month follow-up appointment was scheduled to reappraise progress. A 6-month appointment was also scheduled. James' parents were encouraged to return sooner if they found the techniques were losing effectiveness or if they had specific questions about discipline or behavior.

With regard to medication, James remained on the 10 milligrams each morning and midday and 5 milligrams each afternoon for 2 years; thereafter, the morning and midday doses were raised to 15 milligrams. His weight was monitored twice yearly, and there were no changes from his prior rate of growth.

MICHELLE: MEDICATION AND SOCIAL SKILLS TRAINING

Few children with ADHD are treated in specialized settings such as university-affiliated medical schools or children's hospitals. However, centers such as these that treat large numbers of children with ADHD offer advantages of specialization. Michelle's case exemplifies two of these advantages.

Michelle was an 8-year-old girl referred to the ADHD Clinic at Phoenix (Arizona) Children's Hospital at the encouragement of her school. At school, she showed the classic array of ADHD symptoms: incomplete work, classroom disruptiveness, impulsivity, poor regard for danger on the playground, and alienation of peers by intrusiveness and nonstop action.

Michelle and her family underwent a thorough assessment by a child psychiatrist and psychologist. Michelle's history was consistent with ADHD, as was her presentation when observed in the office. General teacher- and parent-completed rating forms were in accord with the observation and history. After initial data were collected, the tentative impression was that Michelle probably was affected by ADHD. Consequently, she underwent a more detailed evaluation specifically designed to assess ADHD, and ultimately a carefully controlled Ritalin trial.

First, Michelle was brought to a specially arranged observation room and presented with a set of simple arithmetic problems. Her mother was seated beside her with a set of ADHD rating forms to complete while Michelle worked the arithmetic problems. Michelle was instructed to work without looking around, to remain seated, and to refrain from talking to her mother. She was told that she would be observed by the psychologist stationed behind a one-way mirror. Using the observation procedure discussed in Chapter 3, Michelle was monitored for a 10-minute period. She was found to be "off-task" during 12.5% of that time. This is substantial off-task behavior for such a short observation in a largely distraction-free environment.

Second, rating forms specific to ADHD were completed by Michelle's mother and her classroom teacher. The Phoenix [Arizona] Children's Hospital Clinic uses both the ADHD Rating Scale (one form completed by parents, another completed by the teacher) and the Home and School Situations Questionnaires (see Chapter 5). Michelle was found to have extremely high scores on each of these rating forms. That is, not only was she evidencing severe symptoms, but her problems were apparent in many different settings, both at home and in school. Her mother also completed the Personality Inventory for Children, which resulted in a single elevation: on the hyperactivity scale. These pretreatment observations and ratings of behavior are considered to be crucial to a careful appraisal of medication effects; they document the presence and severity of ADHD symptoms before treatment begins.

Third, Michelle's mother completed the Side Effects Rating Scale questionnaire. This form (see Figure 14.1) lists the most common signs and symptoms that may be reported as side effects of stimulant medication, such as Ritalin. Parents are asked to rate whether any of these are present before medication is prescribed, and, if so, how severe they are. Collecting ratings of possible side effects while the child is medication-free is important. For example, many children have preexisting problems with appetite or insomnia. When their medication-free existence is documented, mistaken beliefs that the medicine caused these problems can be avoided. Michelle's mother rated her as having minor problems with headaches (rating of 3 on a scale of 1–9) prior to treatment. No other symptoms on the side effects questionnaire were checked.

After physical data were collected and the child psychiatrist explained the medication to Michelle's

SIDE EFFECTS RATING SCALE

Name ___Michelle Smith___   Date ___7-10-93___
Person Completing This Form ___Mrs. Smith___

Instructions: Please rate each behavior from 0 (absent) to 9 (serious). Circle only one number beside each item. A zero means that you have not seen the behavior in this child during the past week, and a 9 means that you have noticed it and believe it to be either very serious or to occur very frequently.

Behavior	Absent									Serious
Insomnia or trouble sleeping	⓪	1	2	3	4	5	6	7	8	9
Nightmares	⓪	1	2	3	4	5	6	7	8	9
Stares a lot or daydreams	⓪	1	2	3	4	5	6	7	8	9
Talks less with others	⓪	1	2	3	4	5	6	7	8	9
Uninterested in others	⓪	1	2	3	4	5	6	7	8	9
Decreased appetite	⓪	1	2	3	4	5	6	7	8	9

	0	1	2	3	4	5	6	7	8	9
Irritable		1	2	③	4	5	6	7	8	9
Stomachaches	⊘	1	2	3	4	5	6	7	8	9
Headaches	⊘	1	2	3	4	5	6	7	8	9
Drowsiness	⊘	1	2	3	4	5	6	7	8	9
Sad/unhappy	⊘	1	2	3	4	5	6	7	8	9
Prone to crying	⊘	1	2	3	4	5	6	7	8	9
Anxious	⊘	1	2	3	4	5	6	7	8	9
Bites fingernails	⊘	1	2	3	4	5	6	7	8	9
Euphoric/unusually happy	⊘	1	2	3	4	5	6	7	8	9
Dizziness	⊘	1	2	3	4	5	6	7	8	9
Tics or nervous movements	⊘	1	2	3	4	5	6	7	8	9

Figure 14.1. Michelle's pretreatment ratings on the Side Effects Rating Scale. (From R.A. Barkley [1987]. *Defiant children: A clinician's manual for parent training.* New York: Guilford Press; reprinted by permission.)

259

mother, Michelle was ready for the medication trial. Michelle was initially given a 3-week supply of medication. Each week Michelle was to receive a different dosage of Ritalin. One week the dosage would be 5 milligrams twice per day, another week the dosage would be 15 milligrams twice per day, and a third week the dosage would be a placebo (empty capsule disguised to look like the Ritalin-filled capsules) twice per day. Michelle, her mother, her teacher, and the psychologist performing the observation room—derived ratings of on-task behavior were unaware of which dosage was being consumed each week. They were thus "blinded" to the procedure.

At the conclusion of each week, Michelle returned to the Phoenix [Arizona] Children's Hospital ADHD Clinic. As part of each visit, she again worked arithmetic problems in the observation room, and on-task/off-task ratings were calculated. These ratings helped the professional team to evaluate her attention levels as the medication dosages changed. Likewise, Michelle's mother returned completed rating forms (ADHD Rating Scale and Home Situations Questionnaire) describing the status of her ADHD symptoms for that week (i.e., for that particular dosage of medication). Equivalent forms (ADHD Rating Scale and School Situations Questionnaire) were completed by Michelle's classroom teacher. Finally, her mother completed the Side Effects Rating Scale (see Figure 14.1) each week.

At the end of the 3-week trial, the dosages used each week were revealed, and information was summarized so that decisions about continuing medication and selecting an ongoing treatment dosage (if any) could be made. The results of Michelle's trial are shown in Figure 14.2, allowing a quick appraisal of whether improvement had occurred and which dosage

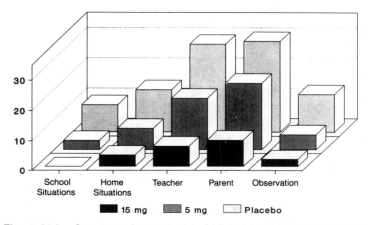

Figure 14.2. Summary of 3-week trial of Michelle's response to controlled Ritalin trial. The lower the ratings on each form, the fewer and less severe the symptoms noted. (School Situations = School Situations Questionnaire; Home Situations = Home Situations Questionnaire; Teacher = Teacher-Completed ADHD Rating Scale; Parent = Parent-Completed ADHD Rating Scale; Observe = in-office observation.)

was most effective. The use of various observations and ratings—some more sensitive to attention, others to conduct and behavior, others to the broad array of ADHD symptoms—helped ensure a thorough investigation of Michelle's symptoms. Michelle responded well to the 15-milligram dosage, and less well but still favorably to the 5-milligram dosage when compared with placebo. She had only slight problems with insomnia, as reflected by the side effects questionnaire ratings, at the two Ritalin dosages. Her headaches did not worsen after medication was started.

Ongoing treatment with 15 milligrams twice a day was agreed to by the child psychiatrist and Michelle's mother. She was scheduled for follow-up visits with the child psychiatrist. Michelle's social problems also received treatment. She was enrolled in a fall and spring sequence (15 sessions each) of group therapy.

With other girls her age, most of whom had social problems, too, Michelle's tendencies to dominate conversations, make disparaging comments, argue abruptly, and flit rapidly from topic to topic were addressed. This group, which was designed to reduce the problems just listed through behavioral techniques, offered important advantages. First, it approximated a natural environment of peers. Immediate feedback, and, if necessary, negative consequences, could follow inappropriate behavior in this setting. Second, acceptable alternative behavior could be taught by using shaping techniques, modeling, and positive feedback (these general techniques are discussed in Chapter 8). Third, parents were enlisted as allies. By noting the behaviors embraced within the group and using similar consequences outside the group, treatment changes could be built upon and their appearance outside the group encouraged.

The combined intervention of medication and social skills training helped Michelle's overall behavior and improved her interaction with her peers. More importantly, her feelings of self-control and self-satisfaction were strengthened.

CONCLUSION

Numerous intervention options are available for children with ADHD. Any individual child may require one or more types of intervention. The most frequently used options include: 1) modification of education services or changes in classroom approach, 2) medication, 3) alternation of techniques of home discipline with increased emphasis on behavior management, and 4) development of social skills in a group therapy format. Parents of children with ADHD should be encouraged by the range of interventions that do exist. Most important is that parents, health practitioners, and school personnel work together closely to ensure that the intervention plans they develop are finely tuned to the child's individual needs and circumstances.

Chapter 15

Financing
Help for Your Child

R ecognizing your child's needs is pointless if you are unable to meet them—you somehow need to finance the services your child requires. What is the best way to accomplish this task? There is no universally correct answer. Your own family's particular circumstances and differences in the service network where you live prevent pat formulas. Nevertheless, this chapter provides some general ideas about the cost of services for your child as well as approaches for financing them.

PUBLIC SCHOOL SERVICES

As stated in Chapter 10, services under the Individuals with Disabilities Education Act (IDEA) or Section 504 of the Rehabilitation Act of 1973 are provided free to parents. Arranging a meeting with school personnel, usually a special education administrator or the school psychologist assigned to your child's school, generally is the first step. Such a meeting may provide you with a sense of the services your child's school is willing to offer. Suspicions that your child has ADHD should generally be shared during this meeting, or an already established diagnosis should be conveyed. Recall also that the school team must themselves establish a diagnosis, or at least concur with a diagnosis from a nonschool professional, before services can be provided. A diagnosis by an outside professional alone is insufficient.

Many schools confine their help for eligible students to classroom adjustments and assistance with academics; that is, they may modify teaching methods or offer tutoring but nothing more. But some schools do offer more, and in rare instances, much more. Social skills training, individual counseling, or parent training are offered by some schools. It is not unheard of for school personnel to arrange for medical consultation or, perhaps, even pay for such services. Even if the school assumes no financial responsibility for nonacademic services, sharing your concerns with them is still wise. They may know the location of free or sliding-scale services; or of which services have good reputations and which don't. Again, situational factors vary. But seeking help from the school is one viable strategy, especially when financial resources are limited.

PUBLIC-SECTOR MENTAL HEALTH SERVICES

Community mental health centers or other facilities committed to the public's mental health are located at many sites in America. These facilities generally render services on a sliding fee basis indexed by a family's ability to pay. Accordingly, fees may be less, sometimes far less, than that paid a private practitioner. If insurance benefits capable of covering services related to ADHD are unavailable for your child, then it may make sense to inquire about community-based mental health programs.

Community mental health programs are not principally concerned with ADHD, nor do they necessarily concern themselves with the education-related problems that often plague children with ADHD. Nonetheless, both ADHD and conduct disorders are common enough that most mental health programs develop some expertise diagnosing and treating these conditions. Many of these programs stress outpatient counseling and psychotherapy, with groups of individuals, whole families, or with the identified individuals themselves. Some programs also offer psychiatric diagnostic services and medication management. School liaison may be provided as well, so that a comprehensive plan can be implemented. Again, individual circumstances vary. You are encouraged to ask school personnel, your child's primary care physician, clergy, or friends about this category of services.

PRIVATE-SECTOR MEDICAL AND BEHAVIOR HEALTH CARE

Private-sector medical and behavior health care encompasses private practitioners and facilities that charge for services, either directly to the family or to the family's health insurance company.

ADHD Clinics and Programs

ADHD clinics and programs are specialized programs that tend to be rare, often confined to medical schools, children's hospitals, or large medical facilities. In these settings extremely specialized medical professionals, such as child psychiatrists or child neurologists, team with professionals from psychology or education to create the intricate diagnostic and treatment services a condition like ADHD requires.

Evaluations in these settings may involve one or more professionals. Typically, rating forms and observation are used, the child and parent are interviewed, and a medical assessment occurs. Depending on the initial reports of the child's school status, a detailed psychoeducational evaluation may or may not be performed. Similarly, a neuropsychological evaluation or even laboratory neurological tests may be conducted for some children. These programs often charge a basic assessment fee, with additional charges incurred only if supplemental testing or laboratory studies are needed. An estimated cost range for this *basic* evaluation is $200–$1,000.

Treatment services vary according to the needs of the child. Of course, large, more-specialized, centers are most apt to provide a full array of services, including services that may be required by only a small percentage of the children they treat. For example, several centers in the United States now offer controlled medication trials. This is a precisely controlled procedure consisting of several weeks' trial on various dosages of medication and the use of a placebo. Rating forms, observation, and the like occur as medication dosages are changed. Fees for this type of service may range from $300 to $500.

Some services and fee ranges of ADHD clinics might include: group therapy and social skills training, $25–$80 per session; individual or family therapy, $75–$150 per session; school visits and consultation, $75–$150 per hour; medication review and physical examination, $25–$60 per quarter hour; parent training, $25–$70 per group session.

Generally, fees reflect the complexity of the service provided, the level and specialization of the provider(s), and the amount of time required to perform the service. Thus, specialized centers that perform complicated procedures with highly trained professionals are likely to be somewhat more expensive than nonspecialized programs. Moreover, some procedures at specialized centers are time consuming (e.g., tabulating of ratings, structured observation of the child while he or she works, or collaboration among several diagnosticians to formulate a treatment plan). This type of service is, understandably, costly.

Psychiatrists and Psychologists

Most child psychiatrists and child psychologists encounter large numbers of children with ADHD, and most are quite accustomed to diagnosing ADHD. A child psychiatrist (M.D. or Doctor of Osteopathy) working alone may charge between $125 and $500 for a complete assessment. He or she may need to refer to a psychologist if a psychoeducational evaluation is required.

A child psychologist working alone may charge between $80 and $400 for a basic evaluation to determine ADHD. If the child is not under the care of a primary care physician (pediatrician or family physician), then an additional referral to rule out medical causes may be required. Both psychiatrists and psychologists, of course, diagnose all sorts of behavior and emotional problems. Their examinations tend to be detailed, in order to rule out other possible mental or behavioral disorders.

Follow-up services may range from approximately $80–$200 per hour for psychiatrists to $65–$150 per hour for psychologists.

Pediatricians, Family Practitioners, and Neurologists

Although not universally true, pediatricians and family practitioners tend to offer less-expensive diagnostic services than specialists. This is true simply because a primary care physician cannot allocate 1 or 2 hours for a single patient. The demands of caring for sick patients preclude it. Less time spent to diagnose your child means smaller charges. Evaluations may range from $40 to $120. Briefer follow-up visits to discuss medication or discipline usually range from $25 to $80. Some pediatricians schedule blocks of time devoted to behavioral or developmental problems. For those who do, appointments tend to be longer, with corresponding increases in professional fees.

Neurologists are specialists rather than primary care physicians, and their fees tend to be higher. A basic evaluation for ADHD probably ranges from approximately $100–$200.

Medication Costs

Medication costs range widely. For the most commonly used medication, Ritalin, children receiving small doses (e.g., 5 milligrams twice per day) may accumulate bills as low as approximately $20 per month. For children requiring larger doses (e.g., 45 milligrams per day) costs are typically in the $50 per month range. Generic medication appears to cost a bit less than name brands; and time-release preparations tend to be a bit more expensive.

Prices vary among the less-frequently-used medications, too (e.g., Cylert or clonidine). Some medications are difficult to obtain without advance notice to your pharmacist. Parents generally find it helpful to shop around or inquire of parents whose children have required medicine for some time. Their experience can be informative.

Health Insurance

The extent to which the preceding services are paid for by health insurance varies greatly. Coverage seems to vary even more for mental health or behavioral health services than for other types of service. Some plans pay a percentage, such as 80%, of "usual and customary" charges. Thus, if a psychiatric consultation were assumed to have a "usual and customary" charge of $200, then the plan would pay $160; patients would shoulder the difference. Families are free to select any provider they like under this arrangement.

Increasingly common is the managed-care option, whereby plan enrollees are directed to specific service providers. Under this arrangement, enrollees typically receive services at fixed (often reduced) rates, or they may make a set copayment (e.g., $15).

Parents seem to encounter three main frustrations with their insurance companies. First, the fee limits can be extremely low. Thus, a company may allow for a psychiatric evaluation, but agree to pay only $55 regardless of the charge; or authorizations for outpatient counseling sessions have caps of $15 per hour. Obviously, such plans leave parents with a large financial burden.

Second, some policies exclude ADHD from coverage. No matter how good the coverage might otherwise be, services to diagnose or treat ADHD will not be reimbursed. The rationale is that ADHD is a developmental or learning problem, not a psychiatric or medical condition.

Third, some managed-care plans do not offer practitioners who are expert in ADHD or in behavioral or developmental problems. For example, none of the available psychiatrists and psychologists in a plan may specialize in treating children.

You are encouraged to consult your company's benefits manual and/or to speak directly to personnel from your company to determine precisely the scope and limitations of benefits relating to ADHD. The need to seek exact information about your particular coverage cannot be overstated. If no acceptable practitioners are listed under your managed-care program, it may be worthwhile to discuss this point with officials from your insurance company. Sometimes modifications can be made.

SUPPORT AND ADVOCACY GROUPS

Many communities have support groups, often created and maintained by parents. Although these groups cannot provide funding for ADHD services, they do help by directing parents to affordable services. They may also assist by advocating for individual children's educational needs. Moreover, problems common to parents of children with ADHD, such as how to discipline, may be examined in meetings of the support group, or through invited speakers, or by distribution of written material. Parents who create their own support network may find that this lessens the need for professional support or advocacy services. Participation in such a group typically involves little or no cost to parents.

Following are the addresses of two national support groups for ADHD. Parents may inquire about local chapters by contacting the national offices.

Children and Adults with Attention Deficit Disorders (CH.A.D.D.)
National Headquarters
Suite 308
499 NW 70th Ave.
Plantation, FL 33317
(305) 587-3700

Attention Deficit Disorders Association (ADDA)
12345 Jones Rd.
Suite 287
Houston, TX 77070
(713) 955-3720

CONCLUSION

Ensuring that your child receives proper services often depends on your knowledge of funding sources and on your insistence that he or she gets that to which he or she is entitled. Hard work and dogged determination may thus be required. Indeed, many parents find that their efforts ultimately pay off and their children's long-term success is enhanced because proper services are secured.

REFERENCES

Abramowitz, A.J., & O'Leary, S.G. (1991). Behavioral interventions for the classroom: Implications for students with ADHD. *School Psychology Review, 20,* 220–234.

Achenbach, T.M., & Edelbrock, C.S. (1983). *Manual for the Child Behavior Checklist and Revised Child Behavior Profile.* Burlington: University of Vermont, Department of Psychiatry.

Acker, M.M., & O'Leary, S.G. (1987). Effects of reprimands and praise on appropriate behavior in the classroom. *Journal of Abnormal Child Psychology, 15,* 549–557.

Ambrosini, P.J. (1987). Pharmacotherapy in child and adolescent major depressive disorder. In H.Y. Meltzer (Ed.), *Psychopharmacology: The third generation of progress* (pp. 1247–1254). New York: Raven Press.

American Psychiatric Association. (1987). *Diagnostic and statistical manual of mental disorders (third edition—revised).* Washington, DC: Author.

August, G.J., & Garfinkel, B.D. (1990). Comorbidity of ADHD and reading disability among clinic-referred children. *Journal of Abnormal Child Psychology, 18,* 29–45.

Barkley, R.A. (1987). *Defiant children: A clinician's manual for parent training.* New York: Guilford Press.

Barkley, R.A. (1990). *Attention deficit hyperactivity disorder: A handbook for diagnosis and treatment.* New York: Guilford Press.

Barkley, R.A. (1991). Diagnosis and assessment of attention deficit-hyperactivity disorder. *Comprehensive Mental Health Care, 1,* 27–43.

Barkley, R.A., & Edelbrock, C.S. (1987). Assessing situation variation in children's behavior problems: The Home and School Situations Questionnaires. In R. Prinz (Ed.), *Advances in behavioral assessment of children and families* (Vol. 3, pp. 157–176). Greenwich, CT: JAI Press.

Barkley, R.A., DuPaul, G.J., & McMurray, M.B. (1991). Attention deficit disorder with and without hyperactivity: Clinical response to three dose levels of methylphenidate. *Pediatrics, 87,* 519–531.

Barkley, R.A., Fischer, M., Edelbrock, C.S., & Smallish, L. (1990). The adolescent outcome of hyperactive children diagnosed by research criteria: I. An 8-year prospective follow-up study. *Journal of the American Academy of Child and Adolescent Psychiatry, 29,* 546–557.

Cantwell, D.P. (1972). Psychiatric illness in the families of hyperactive children. *Archives of General Psychiatry, 27,* 414–417.

Conners, C.K. (1973). Rating scales for use in drug studies with children. *Psychopharmacology Bulletin* [Special issue: Pharmacotherapy with children] *9,* 24–84.

Dulcan, M.K. (1990). Using psychostimulants to treat behavioral disorders of children and adolescents. *Journal of Child and Adolescent Psychopharmacology, 1,* 7–21.

DuPaul, G.J. (1990). *The ADHD Rating Scale: Normative data, reliability, and validity.* Unpublished manuscript, University of Massachusetts Medical Center, Worcester.

Frick, P.J., Kamphaus, R.W., Lahey, B.B., Loeber, R., Christ, M.G., Hart, E.L., & Tannenbaum, L.E. (1991). Academic underachievement and the disruptive behavior disorders. *Journal of Consulting and Clinical Psychology, 59,* 289–294.

Frick, P.J., & Lahey, B.B. (1991). The nature and characteristics of attention-deficit hyperactivity disorder. *School Psychology Review, 20,* 163–173.

Garfinkel, B.D. (n.d.). *Structured ADHD interview: Child version.* Unpublished report, University of Minnesota Medical School, Minneapolis, MN.

Gittelman, R., Mannuzza, S., Shenker, R., & Bonagura, N. (1985). Hyperactive boys almost grown up. *Archives of General Psychiatry, 42,* 937–947.

Gordon, M. (1983). *The Gordon Diagnostic System.* DeWitt, NY: Gordon Systems, Inc.

Green, W.H. (1991). *Child and adolescent clinical psychopharmacology.* Baltimore: Williams & Wilkens.

Greenhill, L.L. (1990). Attention-deficit hyperactivity disorder. In B.D. Garfinkel, G.A. Carlson, & E.B. Weller (Eds.), *Psychiatric disorders in children and adolescents* (pp. 149–182). Philadelphia: W.B. Saunders.

Halperin, J.M., Gittelman, R., Klein, D.F., & Rudel, R.G. (1984). Reading-disabled hyperactive children: A distinct subgroup of attention deficit disorder with hyperactivity? *Journal of Abnormal Child Psychology, 12,* 1–14.

Hartsough, C.S., & Lambert, N.M. (1985). Medical factors in hyperactive and normal children: Prenatal, developmental, and health history factors findings. *American Journal of Orthopsychiatry, 55,* 190–210.

Hinshaw, S.P., Henker, B., & Whalen, C.K. (1984). Cognitive-behavioral and pharmacologic interventions for hyperactive boys: Comparative and combined effects. *Journal of Consulting and Clinical Psychology, 52,* 739–749.

Individuals with Disabilities Education Act Amendments of 1991, PL 102-119. (October 7, 1991). Title 20, U.S.C. 1400 et seq: *U.S. Statutes at Large, 105,* 587–608.

Kendall, P.C. (1985). Toward a cognitive-behavioral model of child psychopathology and a critique of related interventions. *Journal of Abnormal Child Psychology, 13,* 357–372.

Kline, R.G. (1987). Pharmacotherapy of childhood hyperactivity: An update. In H.Y. Meltzer (Ed.), *Psychopharmacology: The third generation of progress* (pp. 1215–1224). New York: Raven Press.

Jacobvitz, D., Sroufe, L.A., Stewart, M., & Leffert, N. (1990). Treatment of attentional and hyperactivity problems in children with sympathomimetic drugs: A comprehensive review. *American Journal of Child and Adolescent Psychiatry, 29,* 677–688.

Lachar, D. (1982). *Personality Inventory for Children: Revised format manual supplement.* Los Angeles: Western Psychological Services.

Lahey, B.B., Pelham, W.E., Schaughency, E.A., Atkins, M.S., Murphy, A., Hynd, G.W., Russo, M., Hartdagen, S., & Lorys-Vernon, A. (1988). Dimensions and types of attention deficit disorder. *Journal of the American Academy of Child and Adolescent Psychiatry 27,* 330–335.

Lambert, N.M., Hartsough, C.S., Sassone, D., & Sandoval, J. (1987). Persistence of hyperactivity symptoms from childhood to adolescence and associated outcomes. *American Journal of Orthopsychiatry, 57,* 22–32.

Lubar, J.F. (1991). Discourse on the development of EEG diagnostics and biofeedback for attention-deficit/hyperactivity disorder. *Biofeedback and Self-regulation, 16,* 202–225.

Mash, E.J., & Johnson, C. (1983). Parental perceptions of child behavior problems, parenting self-esteem, and mothers' reported stress in younger and older hyperactive and normal children. *Journal of Consulting and Clinical Psychology, 51,* 68–99.

Methylphenidate (Ritalin) revisited. (1988). *Medical Letter, 26,* 97–98.

Nichols, P.L., & Chen, T.C. (1981). Minimal brain dysfunction: A prospective study. Hillsdale, NJ: Lawrence Erlbaum Associates.

Rapport, M.D., & Gordon, M. (1987). Attention training system. DeWitt, NY: Gordon Systems, Inc.

Rehabilitation Act of 1973, Section 504, PL 93-112. (1977). Title 29, U.S.C. 791 et seq.

Rosen, L.A., O'Leary, S.G., Joyce, S.A., Conway, G., & Pfiffner, L.J. (1984). The importance of prudent negative consequences for maintaining the appropriate behavior of hyperactive students. Journal of Abnormal Child Psychology, 12, 581–604.

Ross, D.M., & Ross, S.A. (1976). Hyperactivity: Research, theory, and action. New York: John Wiley & Sons.

Sroufe, L.A. (1988, March). Attention deficit hyperactivity disorders in children and adolescents: Assessments and intervention techniques. Unpublished workshop material, Phoenix, AZ.

Teeter, P.A. (1991). Attention-deficit hyperactivity disorder: A psychoeducational paradigm. School Psychology Review, 20, 266–280.

Ullmann, R.K., Sleator, E.K., & Sprague, R. (1984). A new rating scale for diagnosing and monitoring ADD in children. Psychopharmacology Bulletin, 20, 160–164.

Voelker, S.L., Lachar, D., & Gdowski, C.L. (1983). The Personality Inventory for Children and response to methylphenidate: Preliminary evidence for predictive validity. Journal of Pediatric Psychology, 8, 161–169.

Weiner, J.M. (Ed.). (1985). Diagnosis in psychopharmacology of childhood and adolescent disorders. New York: John Wiley & Sons.

Weiss, G. (1991). Attention deficit hyperactivity disorder. In M. Lewis (Ed.), Child and adolescent psychiatry: A comprehensive textbook (pp. 544–561). Baltimore: Williams & Wilkins.

Weiss, G., & Hechtman, L. (1986). Hyperactive children grown up. New York: Guilford Press.

Whalen, C.K., & Henker, B. (1991). Therapies for hyperactive children: Comparisons, combinations, and compromises. Journal of Consulting and Clinical Psychology, 59, 126–137.

Zametkin, A.J., Nordahl, T.E., Gross, M., King, A.C., Semple, W.E., Rumsey, J., Hamburger, S., & Cohen, R.M. (1990). Cerebral glucose metabolism in adults with hyperactivity of childhood onset. New England Journal of Medicine, 323, 1361–1366.

Zentall, S.S. (1989). Attentional cueing in spelling tasks for hyperactive and comparison regular class children. Journal of Special Education, 23, 83–93.

Zentall, S.S., & Dwyer, A.M. (1989). Color effects on the impulsivity and activity of hyperactive children. Journal of School Psychology, 27, 165–173.

Index